Headstate

This volume brings together two plays from author Irvine Welsh. *Trainspotting* was originally published as a novel in 1993 to instant acclaim and has remained on bestseller lists since then. The play was first performed at The Citizens' Theatre, Glasgow, on 23 February 1995. *Headstate*, developed with the Boilerhouse Theatre Company, was first performed at the Lemon Tree Theatre, Aberdeen, on 18 October 1994. Irvine Welsh is also the author of another novel, *Marabou Stork Nightmares*, and a novella, *The Acid House*.

Praise for *Trainspotting*:
'It uses rude words and has the thrill of getting out of your head, being naughty and having a great time. It comes from the Scottish tradition of working-class, stand-up comedy, which laughs at horror.'

Nick Curtis, *Evening Standard*

Praise for *Headstate*:
'*Headstate*, head of state, state of the nation, state of mind, in a state . . . The play aims to capture the essence of Britain after 15 years of Tory rule, but, having been put together over seven weeks with full creative input from director, designer, actors and writer, it's a production in which anything could happen.'

Mark Fisher, *Observer*

WITHDRAWN

THE LEARNING CENTRE
HAMMERSMITH AND WEST

D1375123

HAMMERSMITH AND WEST LONDON COLLEGE

280912

Marabou Stork Nightmares (novel)
The Acid House (novella and short stories)

available from Minerva

Irvine Welsh

Trainspotting
&
Headstate

HAMMERSMITH AND WEST
LONDON COLLEGE
LEARNING CENTRE

0 2 JUL 1996

Minerva

HAMMERSMITH AND WEST
LONDON COLLEGE
LEARNING CENTRE

0 8 JUL 1996

GRE 239097 £5·99
280912
827 WEL

Extracts reproduced from *The Mind Machine* by Colin Blakemore with the permission of BBC Worldwide Limited.

A Minerva Paperback
TRAINSPOTTING & HEADSTATE

First published in Great Britain 1996
as a Minerva original
by Mandarin Paperbacks
an imprint of Reed International Books Ltd
Michelin House, 81 Fulham Road, London SW3 6RB
and Auckland, Melbourne, Singapore and Toronto

Copyright © 1996 by Irvine Welsh
The author has asserted his moral rights

A CIP catalogue record for this title
is available from the British Library
ISBN 0 7493 9573 7

Typeset in Baskerville 10½/11½ by Wilmaset Ltd, Birkenhead, Wirral
Printed in Great Britain by Cox & Wyman Ltd, Reading, Berkshire

This book is sold subject to the condition that it shall not, by way of trade or otherwise, be lent, resold, hired out, or otherwise circulated without the publisher's prior consent in any form of binding or cover other than that in which it is published and without a similar condition including this condition being imposed on the subsequent purchaser.

280912

Contents

Drugs and The Theatre, Darlings

It's a bit trippy writing an intro to *Trainspotting* and *Headstate* as a book of plays, as neither was intended (certainly by me at any rate) to be a play in the first place. I doubted that I would get it together to finish *Trainspotting* as a manuscript for a novel, let alone getting it published or expecting it to take on this life of its own as a classic text for our times without which no home is complete, blah blah. Certainly, I had next to nothing to do with its adaptation for the stage.

Headstate was different, a bigger pain in the arse, in that it involved me actually doing some work, as opposed to my preferred mode of operation, i.e.: sitting back on the sidelines and then springing forth to claim the lion's share of the glory. *Headstate* started life as a series of discussions around some ideas between myself and Boilerhouse Director Paul Pinson. We had a notion to create something that spoke uncompromisingly about who 'we' are and how 'we' got here and it would hopefully be the antithesis of the ugly, smug, bland *Four Weddings And A Funeral* style middle-class escapism which hilariously passes as 'art' today. I was unpublished and unknown at the time and to be upfront I think the main reason Paul wanted to work with me was because I was cheap and Duncan McLean was busy. Anyway, there you go.

Both pieces, for want of a better term, are not drugs pieces, nor are they about drugs. It would be quite shitey if one was simply seen as the smack play and the other as the E play, because that's not really where I'm coming from. This is where I suck in a deep breath and get pompous, but bear with me.

These are pieces about Britain, which, like most Western societies, is a drug society; in so far as most social interaction outside work (although caffeine is the corporate drug) is largely defined by drugs. This has always been the case and, failing a fundamental transformation of society whereby people's imaginative and creative potentials may be fully realised for the common benefit, will invariably remain so.

What to me is significant about Britain is that the 1980s heralded a major change in drug culture. Over this decade, the drugs of choice for many people changed from the state-sponsored poisons of alcohol and tobacco to 'private sector' drugs such as heroin, then Ecstasy and cocaine. Marijuana use also greatly increased over this period, to the extent that the attitude of the state towards it is softening. (Though perhaps not that much, as currently 75% of Britain's imprisoned notorious 'drug dealers' were incarcerated for pushing this killer substance!) Marijuana is a complimentary good to tobacco however. At the time of writing, the current leader of the western world smoked, but did not inhale (aye, right!) this killer plant.

The legal status of drugs has always related to historical, cultural, power and economic factors and has absolutely nothing to do with the health or scientific or criminological issues concerning the toxicity, addictive qualities and social damage caused by a particular drug. The Government in the UK receives massive revenue from the taxation of alcohol and tobacco. The Conservative Party receives sponsorship from corporate drugs barons (Labour would undoubtedly accept the same if offered), this remuneration presumably being paid to continue the physical repression and ideological onslaught against consumer choice in drug use with the current campaigns of disinformation, lies and phoney drugs wars.

The damage to health, the family, society and the economy by the drugs alcohol and tobacco have been well documented. During *Headstate*, a piece of research came to my attention showing that alcohol and tobacco claimed 300,000 lives in Britain per year, while all other drugs could only manage 300. In terms of damage that's AC Milan v. Whitehill Welfare FC. To quote Colin Blakemore, Professor of Physiology at the University of Oxford and a man rightly described by the Royal Society as 'one of Britain's most influential communicators of science':

It is difficult to defend, on logical grounds, a classification of drugs that accepts cigarettes (which are intensely addictive and which kill perhaps a quarter of a million people a week throughout the world) but outlaws marijuana. How can heroin-taking (which simply mimics the actions of a natural chemical in the brain) be wrong, when the consumption of alcohol (which is far more toxic) is right?

(*The Mind Machine*, BBC Publications)

The significant decline in alcohol and tobacco (sales of alcohol have fallen by 11% since 1989) is to do with the increasing availability of superior products. Qualitatively speaking, getting drunk with a group of friends on a pub crawl can be magic, but it pales into insignificance when you get the posse E'd up at a happening event or club. Like alcohol during prohibition, illegal drugs will always flourish and the attendant problems of criminal violence in the drugs scene, poor quality control and above all lack of information and socialisation rituals in drug taking are a direct result of Government policies of illegality and repression. Despite being punished by prison sentences (instead of being rewarded with knighthoods like their counterparts in the brewing, distilling and tobacco industries) drugs entrepreneurs will behave as all entrepreneurs do: they'll take risks for profit.

I personally don't give a fuck whether people choose to use legal or illegal drugs. The main issue for me is that so many people are using drugs negatively, to get as far away from the horror and dullness of straight, mainstream life as possible, rather than positively, as life enhancers. That's the real crime, the real issue; that so many people feel that straight life in this society has so little to offer them. And feel it with such good reason, given the state's constant attacks on its populace, particularly young and old working-class people, over the last two decades.

The main purpose of these notes is not to criticise western drugs policy, although I hope the reader will forgive my rantings as these policies ensure that a lot of people die of ignorance, from misuse of both legal and illegal drugs. But these policies and, more importantly, the deliberate fostering of political, social and economic inequities have altered our various cultures in Britain and that's what informs the two pieces in this book.

The increasing marginalisation and criminalisation of people by the state has resulted in the development of a particular 'alternative' culture and attendant sub-cultures. These cultures are now no longer the preserve of a bohemian few. They are now 'mainstream' in terms of the number of people participating in them, although you would never learn this through the popular media. They are also 'underground', precisely because of this state criminalisation and therefore are only, if they are deemed to exist at all, given the most tentative and low-key coverage. They only shoot to prominence when an extreme situation, for example, an 'Ecstasy-related' death, allows 'moral panic' to be generated. The generation of such 'moral panic' is almost always a prerequisite for more repressive social control measures. Those in the business of generating such 'moral panic' and clamouring for further repression might be better served in asking why there have been fifty 'Ecstasy-related deaths' in Britain, but only one in the Netherlands. The differing attitudes in these societies to drugs information and drug use is undoubtedly the key to this. It might also be useful to compare this figure to the number of young people who die every year from 'alcohol-related' causes. These are the most common types of drugs deaths but the legality and wide availability of alcohol is, of course, defended on the grounds of 'freedom of choice' in that people have always, and will always, periodically abuse alcohol.

For me, the most important way of making sense of British culture is to see it in terms of pre and post acid house culture. This, for me, has absolutely fuck all to do with musical preferences, clothes, and only really consequentially (though significantly) to do with lifestyle and drug choices. I think it's to do with reclaiming the entrepreneurial spirit towards creativity, expression and enjoyment of life for its own sake, rather than simply personal profit. It's both a reaction against the narrow individualism as defined by the political right (the reduction of the individual to a mere consumer who makes qualitatively meaningless choices from a selection of trinkets presented to them by those who hold power) and a move towards the collective interactions destroyed by 1980s industrial closures and community devastations, anti-union legislation and even the Taylor report on football stadia which means that the only way working-class people can now meaningfully interact is in clubs, at raves and at parties. In the words of the poet Paul Reekie, 'the chill-out zones are the new bootcamps of interaction'. The emasculation of the collective is the real reasoning behind the Criminal Justice Bill, possibly the most Orwellian entitled piece of legislation ever, as it's actually concerned with promoting both criminality and injustice. However, far from being a simple rejection of individualism, house culture is about broadening the basis of that individualism. It is about individual spirituality, about attempting to understand the entire psychic terrain an individual operates in. It'll never be recognised as such: the bourgeois cultural fascists of the media and arts establishments could never bring themselves to concede that an eighteen-year-old unemployed person with a set of decks and some good friends might be far more adept at exploring their social and spiritual identity than they could ever hope to be.

. While the shock tactics of 'political' punk ended up an advertiser's boon (think of United Colors of Benetton), what underpinned its petulant 'you're boring old farts' sneer, was 'we can do better'. John Lydon's still saying: 'now open up'. No problem, come on in. Ad agencies, the media, etc., they all said it: 'come on in and shake us up'. The subtext was: 'and stick around until you sound twice as pathetic as the hippies you once mocked.' On the other hand, 'non-political' house has been underground since 1988 and is moving faster than a market which had all but swallowed up and shat out its posturing predecessor within a few years. The society we live in can now no longer offer the mass of its citizens secure, well-paid work, and organisations are demanding more and more from people for less and less. However, many people are less concerned with 'getting in and getting on' (as if it was either a desirable, or indeed, a possible option for many) as with 'doing their own thing', to reclaim that admittedly cringeworthy sixties phrase. People I have a great deal of respect for, the writer Duncan McLean, and the actor Tam Dean Burn, have said of literature and theatre that they need their punk revolution. While I can appreciate the sentiments behind these comments, I'd beg to differ. Writing and theatre need a punk revolution like I need a pint of McEwans Lager.

Trainspotting was started as a novel in the summer of 1988, though parts of it originated in notes and scenarios I wrote to alleviate the boredom of a New York–Los Angeles Greyhound Bus journey some years earlier. In the summer of 1988 I was dancing in the fields looking up at the sun, off my face on the first batch of Ecstasy to hit Britannia's shores.

Bullshit. Chance would have been a fine thing.

I was sitting in Heriot-Watt University's library, where I had been sent by my employer to 'study' for the yuppie Dazcoupon qualification they call the MBA. (Master's degree in business administration.) I was packed into a lecture theatre with forty other sponsored employees and the only repetitive beats I got into my skull that summer were those of the bottom line rather the bass line. At this point I'd better add that just in case anyone thinks that the schemie was obviously bitter at having been found wanting with the intellectual demands and academic rigour required by the post-graduate programme, I passed effortlessly. I was bored and had time on my hands, so I started to write *Trainspotting*. I appreciated the sponsorship by my employer: it served the purpose of getting me away from work for a bit. While I was writing in the library I discovered that quantitative methods and cost accountancy weren't really what I wanted to do. What I wanted to do was to express my anger at the death of people where I grew up.

It was listening to a fellow MBA student from the Home Counties and a middle-class Glaswegian student telling me about what kind of a city Edinburgh was that made me think about its image. That image, that of the middle-class, festival city, was at worst a lie and at best perversely one-sided. Yet it had a hegemony over all the other images of this urban, largely working-class but multi-cultural city. Other realities existed, had to be shown to exist.

It's inevitable that this has happened, largely as a result of what is usually referred to as 'the importance of tourism to the local economy'. Tourists want to come to the Athens of the North rather the HIV capital of Europe. Nothing wrong in that. But the people who suffer from HIV (and all the other inhabitants of Edinburgh's outlying housing schemes) are therefore deemed detrimental to tourism, which, of course is staggeringly important to the local economy. So the schemes are kept out. Out of sight, out of mind. Out of range of resource allocation for vital services like health and housing. Maybe I was just a wee bit blinkered when I was growing up in Muirhouse, but I failed to notice the benefits of tourism to the local economy. Understandably, there's a time-lag in the 'trickle-down' wealth effect, much advocated by right-wing economists, but twenty-odd years? Get to fuck. Who is benefiting from tourism if it isn't Muirhouse? Probably Niddrie, Wester Hailes or Oxgangs . . . not.

Edinburgh's 'affluence' (if you didn't count the schemes and Edinburgh most certainly didn't), was there for all to see in its neat and clean city centre. Other cities, their traditional industries dismantled in the seventies and eighties, cottoned on to this long-standing scam. The Glasgow City of Culture idea basically followed this formula: reinvent the city by tarting up its centre, but only its centre, and forget the schemes. Other cities in Britain followed suit. Now most British city centres that escaped the ugliness of sixties redevelopment look very nice, but such places are not for the schemes. They are for yuppie incomers, shoppers and tourists. The 'city' (the city-centre) is for this alliance of new bourgeois and old bourgeois, and so therefore, is its 'art'. It has to be 'life-affirming', or, more accurately, re-affirming of those liberal middle-class values that everything and everyone is really rather jolly decent and wonderful.

Fuck that for a laugh; if we're truly a diverse multi-cultural society, (and we are) let's have some diverse, multi-cultural art and art criticism.

The Citizen's Theatre in Glasgow staged the first production of *Trainspotting*. It was directed by Ian Brown of the Traverse Theatre in Edinburgh. Harry Gibson dramatised the book with tremendous empathy and Ian assembled a brilliant cast in Susan Vidler, Jim Cunningham, Malcolm Shields and Ewen Bremner. As I said, I had little to do with this production. I thought it appropriate that someone fresh handled it to see what they could do with it. I did a reading for the cast and chatted to them about the characters, and basically that was me. The cast and Ian Brown were as cool as fuck, so I knew that it was going to be good. I was unprepared for how good. It blew me away. Ian took it to London and Harry assembled another cast and took it around the country. It's off. The play has a life of its own. As I write, it's being made into a film. Apart from a small bit of acting and a few discussions with the producer, director and screenwriter, I've taken the same hands-off approach, to the obvious benefit of the film, which is magic.

Headstate had a very different life. We wanted to assemble a collaborative team and work on a piece that would be very different from the potential 'long-running play' of *Trainspotting*. The idea about this was that it would be a snapshot of a point in time (now) looking at what formed 'our' (how many questions does that word raise?) current sensibilities over the last fifteen or so years. Everyone in the team assembled came with their own agenda, and I suppose mine was to look at what the writer Kodwo Eshun termed 'post-rave burnout'. I was initially suspicious of the idea of the 'last fifteen years' concept, because the last thing I wanted to get involved in was a narrow bitter polemic about 'Tory misrule' or 'monetarism' or 'Thatcherism', mainly because all those things actually started in 1976, not 1979, when the Labour Government expressly went to the institutions of multi-national capitalism with a programme for the domestic economy based on those principles. Now, under Blair's leadership, they seem set to carry them forward with renewed vigour as the Tories have ran out of steam.

Paul Pinson brought the actors Jan Knightley, Tam Dean Burn, Rachael Gartside and dancer/performer Christine Devaney as well as designer Karen Tennent, and lighting designer George Tarbuck to the project. My contribution to the personnel situ was to get a friend from London involved in doing the music, Graham Cunnington who is a brilliant musician and a founder member of Test Department. Whatever else happened, I knew the music would be top notch. It was, but so was everything else.

I saw *Headstate* as more of a pre-club night rather than a piece of theatre. My concept was for punters to come along, neck a pill, get into it, then head off to a club. If I was doing something like this again, I'd probably want it to take place in a club venue rather than theatrical/performance space. This isn't a slag-off at the venues who gave us magnificent help and co-operation, more a bitch at the rigidity of arts funding that says something has to be 'this' or 'that' and you have to jump through the appropriate hoops.

I was excited at the prospect of working with Jan and Tam who I had seen in action prior to us getting together, and who I knew to be superb performers and dangerously committed to seeking out uncomfortable truths. We got together with Chrissie and Rachael and as they say in the cliché, 'forged a common vision' (or as common a vision as possible) and most importantly, had a good time in the devising process, with loads of partying (purely for research, of course) flung into the equation. Tam Dean Burn is still in role even as I write, eight months on. It was a cool as fuck time despite my own head being in a bit of a state as I had just finished writing a novel (*Marabou Stork Nightmares*) and probably could have done with not really thinking about anything else. I was also in the process of moving from Edinburgh to Amsterdam. Karen, George and Graham created a magnificent environment, without which the play couldn't be performed and record companies are devoid of any sense at all if they don't bring out Graham's piece of music; they should be contract-killing each other for it. The environment was absolutely essential. This is a way of saying to all theatre groups: think very carefully before you try this at home.

One more point about writing this introduction in Amsterdam is that I'm not writing it in Britain. *Headstate* could only have happened in Britain. In Holland there isn't the same level of oppression to kick back against, and nice one to the Dutch for that. (As I write this I'm aware that some people, particularly those who originate from the old Dutch colonies, may beg to differ, perhaps after visiting the Alienspolice at the Bijlmer to register.) I'll borrow the words of Dutch underground libertarian polemicist Nils Van Smeets: WHEN FREEDOM IS OUTLAWED ONLY THE OUTLAWS CAN BE FREE. In other words: fuck the cunts, they know who they are and so do we. Just fuck them.

Irvine Welsh, Amsterdam, July 1995

Trainspotting

adapted for the stage by Harry Gibson from the novel by Irvine Welsh

This version of *Trainspotting* was first performed at The Edinburgh Festival, on 11 August 1995, and later on national tour in 1995, and at London's Ambassador's and Whitehall Theatres in 1996 with the following cast:

Mark	Paul Ireland
Tommy	Peter J. Ireland
Franco	Gavin Marshall
Alison	Gayanne Potter and Michelle Gomez

Director Harry Gibson
Designer Suzanne Field
Lighting Michael Lancaster

Earlier versions were performed at The Citizens' Theatre, Glasgow, and The Traverse Theatre, Edinburgh, in 1994, and at The Citizens' Theatre in 1995, with different casts. A fourth production toured Britain in 1996.

Characters

Mark (Boy in Pub)
Tommy (Sick Boy / Drunk)
Franco (Mr McKay / Johnny)
Alison (June / Lassie in Pub / Lizzie)

Part One

1

Mark Fuck!. . .

Ah woke up in a strange bed, in a strange room, covered in ma own mess. Ah hud pished the bed. Ah hud puked up in the bed. Ah hud shat masel in the bed. Ah slide outay bed. Ah pick up the duvet. Ah look down. The bed is a total fucking mess. The wee pink carnations on a white background're drownin in toxic brown pollution. I huv tae gather it up in the bottom sheet like chips in a paper and then wrap it up in the duvet cover, sortay crush it intae a ball, makin sure thir's nae leakage, ken, and stow it under the bed. Then ah turn the mattress ower tae hide the damp patch. Then ah see masel in a mirror. Jesus Christ! Ah steal ootay the bedroom intae the toilet tae shower the crap aff my chest, thighs n erse. The toilet is – nice. Who the fuck dae ah know with a nice toilet? O no. Gail Houston! Ah'm in Gail Houston's mother's hoose. How did ah get here? Whae brought us here? Who the fuck undressed us? Ah remember fuck all eftir the pub in Rutherglen.

Where Gail Houston came intae the picture ah'm no awfy sure. Wid been goin oot fir six weeks but wid no had sex. She hud said she did not want oor relationship tae start oot oan a physical basis, as that wid be how it wid principally be defined fae then on in. She hud read this in *Cosmopolitan*, ken. So six weeks oan ah've got a pair of bollocks like watermelons. There was probably a fair bit of spunk in that bed alongside the pish, shite n puke. Anyway, ah've just goat doon under the bare duvet on the bare mattress hopin fir a wee bit sleep when the door opens. Gail comes intae the room. It is morning. 'You were in some state last night then!' she says. 'What happened to the bed covers?' 'Eh, a wee accident, Gail.' Ahm no sure she completely understands but ahm no wantin tae paint hur a picture. She wrinkles her nose and says tae niver mind n come doonstairs 'wir just goannae huv some breakfast'. She sweeps out. Breakfast?! Ah get up n get dressed n creep doon the stairs – takin ma bundle with me as ah want tae take it hame and get it cleaned. Ken?

Right. Gail's parents are sitting at the kitchen table. The sounds n smells ay a traditional Sunday breakfast fry-up are un-fuckin-speakable. 'Well, someone was in a state last night,' says Gail's Ma, but teasingly ken. Ah flush wi embarrassment. Mr Houston, sitting at the kitchen table, tries tae smooth things ower fir us. 'Ah well,' sais he, 'it does ye good tae cut loose once in a while.' 'It would do this one good tae be tied up once in a while,' sais Gail. (Wee bit bondage wid dae me fine.) 'Eh, Mrs Houston,' ah sais, pointing tae ma carryoot, 'ah made a bit ay a mess ay the sheet n the duvet cover. Ah'm going tae take thum home n clean thum. Ah'll bring thum back tomorrow.' 'Aw, don't you worry about that, son. Ah'll just stick them in the washing machine.' (She does not understand.) 'You sit down and get some breakfast.' 'Naw, but, eh, a really bad mess. Ah feel embarrassed enough. Ah'd like tae take them home.' 'Dearie dear!' Mr Houston laughs – uncomprehendingly. 'Now no, you sit down, son, ah'll see tae them' – Mrs Houston steals across the flair taewards us n makes a grab fir ma bundle. She widnae be denied. Ah pull it tae me, tae my chest; but Mrs Houston is fast as fuck n deceptively strong. She got a good grip and pulled against me. The sheets flew up in the air – n a pungent shower ay shite, alcoholic sick n vile pish splashed oot across the scene. Mrs Houston stands mortified, for a few seconds before runnin heavin tae the sink. Brown flecks ay runny shite sit oan Mr Houston's glasses, face n white shirt. 'God sake, god sake,' Mr Houston croaks . . . as Mrs Houston boaks, and ah'm tryin tae mop some ay the mess back intae the sheets . . . Ah never did get hur intae bed eftir that.

2

Tommy   Hey!

Mark   Tommy!

Tommy   Mind the time ah went wi Laura McEwan?

Mark   Laura McEwan?! A girl wi an awesome sexual reputation.

Tommy   One night in a Grassmarket pub she jist grabs me and takes me hame. She says, 'Ah want you tae take ma erse virginity. Fuck me in the erse. Ah've nivir done it that wey before.' 'Eh' (ah sez) 'yeah, that sounds barry . . .' But there were some other things she wanted tae dae wi me first. She binds ma ankles thegither wi sellytape. Wuv nae claes oan ken. Wuv stripped oaf. Ah'm leyin oan the bed. Right. She's bound ma ankles thegither wi sellytape. An, uh, ma wrists. She's bound them wi sellytape an aw.

Mark   So how you gaunnae fuck er in the erse if ye don't mind ma askin?

Tommy   She sais 'Ah'm daein this because ah don't want ye tae hurt me, understand? We do it fae the side.'

Mark   Fuck off!

Tommy   'The minute ah start tae feel pain it's fuckin ower. Right? Because naebody hurts me. No fuckin guy ivir hurts me. Ye understand me?' 'Yeah, sound, likesay, sound . . .' Ah dinnae want tae hurt enywan. Enywey, ah'm lying there, trussed up oan the bed, naked likes, n she's rubbing her crotch n seyin 'You're beootiful!' Ah'd nivir been telt before that ah wis beautiful. She gies us a blaw job. Whoooo . . . awwww! N then, just before ah was about tae come, she stoaps. N she leaves the room. She leaves me lyin there, tied up wi sellytape and a dick like a pickaxe-handle. Ah started tae get a wee bit paranoid. Laura hud a longterm partner called Roy committed tae a psychiatric hoaspital. She comes back in the bedroom n she's goat somethin in her hond. 'Ah want you to dae us in the arse now. So ah'm gaunnae vaseline your dick heavily so that it doesnae hurt me when you put it in. My muscles'll be tight, cause this is new tae me, but ah'll try tae relax.' She's smokin a jint at the time. Mebbe a bit stoaned. Cos it wisnae Vaseline she found in the bathroom cupboard, it was Vick's Vapour Rub. Aaaaaargh! Ah thought the tip ay ma penis hud been sliced oaf. 'Fuck. Sorry,' she sais. She helps us oaf the bed, she helps us intae the toilet, ah was hoppin along shedding tears ay pain, she's fillin the sink wi water . . . And then she's leaving the room tae find a pair of scissors tae cut the fuckin sellytape. Ah struggled up oan the sink and lowered ma cock in the water. Fuck. Ah woke up in hoaspital. Ah'd six stitches in ma heid, sellytape burns oan ma ankles n a hoat dog between ma legs. So don't you greet ower Gail Houston, coz ah nivir did get tae fuck the erse aff Laura McEwan.

3

Mark   Whit dae ye dae?

Tommy   Get a joab?

Mark   Fuckoff. Ah'm happy steying oan the rock'n'roll.

Tommy   How many places is it yur signin oan at now?

Mark   One in Edinburgh, one in Glasgow, three in London. Five. Keepin up wi it's a full-time joab. Plus they're gaunnae send ye fir a real joab fae time tae time, so there's interviews tae fuck up.

Tommy   Thuv sent me fir a joab –

Mark   Bastards.

Tommy   – in a hotel. (*Passes* **Mark** *a slip of paper.*)

Mark   Fuckin bastards.

Tommy   Ah seen it. Looks like a fuckin palace.

Mark   Porterin?!

Tommy   Ah'll fuck it up.

Mark   Aye, but ye've goat tae fuck it up carefully, ken?

Tommy   If we jist be oorselves n be honest, like, say 'This is me', ken? Thill nivir gie either ay us a joab, ivir.

Mark   Naw, see, if yir too obvious the cunts'll tell the dole n the bastards stoap yir giro. Thill say 'That joabseeker jist cannae be bothered tae seek a joab!'

Tommy   Fuck. Whit am ah gaunnae dae?

Mark   Remember whit school ye went tae?

Tommy   Ah went tae Leithy, man, same as you.

Mark   Naw, see oan the fuckin application form ye pit doon that ye went tae a posh school, George Heriot's or that –

Tommy   George Heriot's?!

Mark   Because it's a wellknown fact that ye nivir stand a fuckin chance ay getting anything *decent* in this city if ye didnae go tae a posh school.

Tommy   But . . . see . . .

Mark   But – no way will they offer a George Heriots man a fuckin *porterin joab in a hotel*. That's only fir us plebs. If they see Leithy or Craigy oan your form, the cunts'll gie ye the joab. See.

Tommy   Uh . . .

Mark   In fact, ah did attend George Heriot's, whin ah wis an apprentice joiner. We went tae build some shelves.

Tommy   Right!

Mark   Ah'll show ye how it's done.

McKay   Sit yourself down, Mr Renton. I see from your application form that you attended George Heriots.

Mark   Right. Seems like a long time ago now.

McKay   Old McDonald still doing his rounds?

Mark   God you're taking me back now.

McKay   Aye . . . Good Man . . .

Mark   Fuck. He's happy wi that. He likes me. The cunt is gonnae offer us the joab. Ma theory is fucked. This is terrifying. Ah've goat tae dae somethin here.

McKay   Ehm . . . Mark . . . ehm . . . can you ehm . . . explain the ehm . . . the gaps . . . in your employment record?

Mark   (Can you explain the gaps in your speech, ya cunt?)
Ehm . . . Mr McKay . . .

McKay   Aleister.

Mark   Aleister . . . I've had a long-standing problem with
heroin addiction. I've been trying to combat this, but it has
curtailed my employment activities. I feel it's important to
be honest and mention this to you, as a potential future
employer. (See me shooting up in yer hotel lavvies and
selling mah erse tae your guests?)

Mark *and* **Tommy**   (No way!)

McKay   Well, eh, thank you for being so frank with us, Mr
Renton. Eh, we do have some other people to see . . . so
thanks again and we'll be in touch.

Mark   Magic. See, act enthusiastic. Sell yirself . . . and then
tell the truth . . .

Tommy   Right man. But it's hard fir me, man, ken? Ah get
pure shy, ken?

Mark   Here. This'll buck ye up a bit.

Tommy   Whit's this?

Mark   Speed. Guid stuff. Davie Mitchell gied us it. It'll let
ye sell yirself.

Tommy   Whoah! Ah feel dynamic. Like, ah'm really intae
this interview. Like ye say sell yirself n tell the truth.

Mark   Aye . . .

Tommy   You n me, man. Let's do it.

McKay   Sit yourself down – Mr Murphy.

Tommy   Whoah!

McKay   I see from your application form that you
attended George Heriots. The Old Boys seem to be rather
thick on the ground this afternoon.

Tommy   Actually man ah've goat tae come clean here. Ah
went tae Augie's, St Augustine's likesay, then Craigy, eh

Craigroyston, ken. Ah jist pit doon Heriots because ah thoat it wid likes help us git the joab. Too much discrimination in this town, man, ken, likesay? As soon as suit n tie dudes see Heriots or Edinburgh Academy they get the hots, ken. Ah mean, would you have said likesay 'ah see you attended Craigroyston'?

McKay   Well I was just making conversation, as I did happen to attend Heriots myself. The idea was to make you feel at ease. But I can certainly put your mind at rest with regards to discrimination. That's all covered in our equal opportunities statement.

Tommy   It's cool man, ah'm relaxed, it's jist that ah really want this joab likesay, couldnae sleep last night, worried ah'd sortay blow it likesay, ken? It's jist when cats see 'Craigroyston' oan the form they likesay think well everybody thit went tae Craigie's a waster, right? But . . .

McKay   Well, I —

Tommy   . . . ye ken Scott Nisbet the fitba player likesay, he's in the Huns, eh Rangers first team, haudin his ain against aw they expensive international signins ken? That cat wis the year below us at Craigie, man.

McKay   I can assure you Mr Murphy —

Tommy   Tommy.

McKay   — we're far more interested in the qualifications you gained rather than which school you, or any other candidate, went to.

Tommy   Hey whatever you say man. You're the man, the governor, the dude in the chair so tae speak likesay.

McKay   Now, it says here that you got five O grades — Sociology, Food & Nutrition, Fabric & Fashion —

Tommy   Whoah. Likesay, gaunnae huv tae stop ye thair catboy. The O grades wis bullshit, ken? Thought ah'd use that tae git ma fit in the door. Showin initiative, likesay. Ken? Ah really want this joab man, ah —

McKay   Why do you want this job so desperately that you're prepared to lie?

Tommy   Ah need the hireys man.

McKay   The what?

Tommy   The poppy, likesay, the bread, the dosh n that. Ken?

McKay   Thank you very much, Tommy, we'll let you know.

Tommy   Naw, man, the pleasure wis mine. Best interview ah've been at, ken?

Mark   So how'd it go Tam?

Tommy   Ah think they might be gaunnae offer us the joab.

Mark   Fuck!

Tommy   Fuck!! One thing though man, ye wir right aboot this speed, it really helps ye sell yirself.

Mark   Another dab?

Tommy   Wouldnae say naw, man, would not say no likes.

4

Mark   Ah've had a longstanding problem wi heroin addiction. Ah've bin trying tae combat this but it has curtailed ma employment activities. I feel it's important tae be honest and mention this tae you . . .
Ye become restless n uneasy, weak n irritable, yur nose n eyes start tae run, yur yawnin, yur tremblin, sweatin n sneezin. Yur limbs ache n yur pupils dilate. Yur ootay yir box.
Right. We're in ma flat. Wir watching a – Who the fuck was wi me? No Tommy. He wisnae intae the skag. Sick Boy! Simon Sick Boy Williamson! We cried him Sick Boy no coz he was eywis sick wi junk withdrawal but because he's jist one sick cunt.
Wir watching a Jean-Claude van Damme video.

Simon   But what wir waiting fir is another fukken fix, a trip tae see the Mother Superior, fukken quick an aw.

Mark   Wir gettin sick. But ah'm hangin in thair, waiting fur Jean-Claude tae get doon tae some serious swedgin.

Simon   Mark. Ah've goat tae see Mother Superior.

Mark   Sick Boy was bad. The sweat was lashin ofay him; he wis trembling. Ah wis focussin oan the telly, trying no tae notice the cunt. He wis bringin us doon.

Simon   Maaark!

Mark   Aw, haud oan a second.

Simon   Ah've goat tae fuckin move, man!

Mark   Ah wanted tae see Jean-Claude smash the fuckin –

Simon   Let's fuckin go!

Mark   Fuckin waste. Ah willnae get to watch it now.

Simon   Ye can watch it the night.

Mark   'sdue back now. Thull gie us back-charges at the shoap.

Simon   Fucksake, ah'll gie ye the money tae get it back oot. Fifty measley fuckin pence.

Mark   That's no the fuckin point.

Simon   The point is ah'm really fuckin suffering here – and yur draggin yur feet deliberately.

Mark   Ah'm no!

Simon   Fling yer fuckin jaykit oan well!

5

Simon   Supposed tae be a fuckin taxi rank here.

Mark   Supposed to be fuckin August but ah'm fuckin freezin mah baws oaf here. Ah'm no sick yet, but ah can feel it coming, it's in the fuckin post, that's fir sure.

Simon   The taxis are aw up curb-crawlin fur rich
Edinburgh Festival cunts too fuckin lazy tae walk a hundred
fuckin yards fae one poxy church hall tae another fir thir
fuckin drama shows.

Mark   Simon!

Simon   Money-grabbin bastards . . .

Mark   These guys, Simon, ah think . . .

Simon   Lowest form ay vermin oan god's earth.

Mark   These boys huv been waiting fur taxis afore us, Si –

Simon   Taxii!!!

Mark   He charges straight oot intae the middle ay the
Walk screaming, 'Taxi!' and a guy in a black, purple n aqua
shell-suit shouts, 'Whit's the fuckin score?'

Simon   Fuck off, ya plukey-faced wee hing oot. Git a
fuckin ride! Cummon Mark! Tollcross mate.

Mark   'Cummon ye crappin bastards!'

Simon   Cummon!

Mark   We piled intae the taxi. Gob splattered against the
side windae. The driver wasnae amused. See what yuv done
now, ya big-moothed cunt? Next time one ay us ur walking
hame on ur Jack Jones, wi get hassle fae these wee radges.

Simon   Yir no feart ay they wee fuckin saps ur ye?

Mark   Aye, aye ah fuckin am if ah'm oan ma tod n ah git
set oan by a fuckin squad ay shell-suits. Ye think ah'm Jean-
Claud van Fuckin Damme? Fuckin doss cunt –

Simon   Ah want tae see Mother Superior n ah dinnae gie a
fuck aboot any cunt else. Goat that? Watch ma fuckin lips –

Mark   Wir here.

Simon   Boot fuckin time.

6

Mark Up there was Johnny Swan, Swanney. We cried him 'Mother Superior' because of the length of time he'd had his habit.

As we hit the stairs tae Johnny's gaff, ah was staring tae get bad cramps. Soon ah'm dripping like a saturated sponge wi the effort ay climbing the stairs. Sick Boy wis probably worse, but the cunt was beginning no tae exist fir us. Ah cud hear him up ahead ay me, struggling fir breath. At the topay the stair ah find him slouched against the banister blocking ma route tae Johnny's door, ma route tae the skag. 'Awright Si?' ah sais, pissed off at the cunt fir haudin us up. Ah thought he wis gaunnae spew intae the stairwell. He waves us away, shaking his heid and screwing his eyes up. Ah sais nae mair. Whin ye feel like he did, ye dinnae want tae talk or be talked at. Ye dinnae want any fuckin fuss at aw. Ah didnae either. Sometimes ah think people become junkies just because they crave a bit ay silence. The doorbell was shatterin. Johnny Swan was bombed outay his box.

Johnny Ahaww! Ah've goat wan Sick Boy here an another sick boy there an that makes two sick fuckin boeys!

Mark He'd once been a really good mate ay mines, back in the auld days. We played fitba thegither fir Porty Thistle. Now he's just a dealer. He sais tae us once, 'Nae friends in this game. Jist associates.' Ah thought he was being show-oafy, until ah got sae far intae the skag. Now ah ken precisely what the cunt means. The piss-heid in the pub wants every cunt tae git as ootay it as he is, the real junky doesnae gie a fuck aboot emdy else. Nae friends . . .

Alison *enters.*

Mark Alison was thair. Ye wir thair. Alison wis cookin. Sick Boy wis sittin up cloas tae her, never taking his eyes oaf the contents ay the spoon she wis heatin over a candle. Johnny bends doon in front ay Sick Boy, pulls his face tae him and kisses him, hard, on the lips. Sick Boy pushes him away, trembling. 'Fuck off! Doss cunt!' cries the sick boy.

Simon   Doss cunt!

Mark   Johnny n Ali laugh, loudly. O, ah wid huv laughed loudly n aw, if ah hudnae felt each bone in ma body wis being crushed in a vice n set aboot wi a blunt hacksaw. Sick Boy picked up the leather strip and tourniquayed Ali above her elbow, obviously staking his place in the queue, and then tapped up a big blue vein oan her thin ash-white airm.

Simon   Want me tae dae it?

Mark   She nodded. Alison nodded. He droaps a cotton ball intae the spoon n blaws oan it, before sucking up aboot 5 mls through the needle, intae the barrel ay the syringe. He's goat a fuckin huge blue vein tapped up, which seems tae been almost coming through Ali's airm. He pierces her flesh and injects a wee bit slowly, before sucking blood back intae the chamber. Her lips are quivering as she gazes pleadingly at him for a second or two . . . His face looks ugly, leering, reptilian, before he slams the cocktail towards her brain! She pulls back her heid, shuts her eyes and opens her mooth, givin oot an orgasmic groan. She sais . . . She sais . . .

Alison   That beats any meat injection. That beats any fuckin cock in the world!

Mark   Aye. Sick Boy's eyes are now innocent and full ay wonder, his expression like a bairn thit's come through oan Christmas morning tae a pile ay gift-wrapped presents stacked under a tree. Simon and Alison baith look strangely beautiful and pure in the flickering candlelight. 'That beats any meat injection. That beats any fucking cock in the world'. Then Johnny helps Sick Boy tae cook up and shoot home. Just as Sick Boy is aboot tae scream, Johnny spikes a vein, draws some blood back intae the barrel, and fires the life-giving and life-taking elixir home. Sick Boy hugs Swanney tightly . . . then eases off, keeping his airms aroond him. They were relaxed, like lovers in a post-coital embrace. Then ah went tae take a shoat. It took us ages tae find a good vein. Ma boys don't live as close tae the surface as maist people's. When it came, ah savoured the hit. Ali wis right. Take yir best orgasm, multiply the feeling by twenty, and

you're still fucking miles off the place. Ma dry cracking bones
are soothed and liquefied by ma beautiful heroine's tender
caresses. Alison and Sick Boy got up n trooped outay the
room thegither.

Alison *and* **Simon** *leave.*

Mark   They looked bored and passionless, but when they
didnae come back, ah knew that they'd be shagging in the
bedroom.
What dae ye dae. . . ?

Alison *returns screaming.*

Mark   Alison comes back intae the room screamin.
It's horrible. Ah cannae handle this.

Alison (*incoherent*)   The bairn's away, the bairn's away.
Dawn . . . oh my god . . . o fucking god.

Mark   We ken thit something really bad has happened
because Alison has come ben the room, screamin!

Alison (*incoherent*)   Dawn. O my god. O fuckin god.

Mark   Johnny moves ontae the couch, sittin a few feet fae
Alison. Her heid's in her hands. Ah thought that he wid
touch her. Ah hoped he would. Ah'm willing um tae dae it –
But he jist stares at her. So ah sais . . . ah sais whit ah always
say when somethin bad happens. 'Ah'm cookin up in a bit'.

Alison (*incoherent*)   It's ma fault, it's ma fault, it's ma
fault . . .

Johnny   Eh . . . Ali . . . likesay, Mark's cookin up, eh . . .
ye ken, likesay eh . . . he's um . . . ye shouldnae . . . whit –

Mark   Sick Boy comes back through. His boady's strainin
as if against the limits ay an invisible leash.

Simon   Fuck . . .

Mark   His voice reminds us –

Simon   . . . some fuckin life, eh?

Mark   – ay the demon in *The Exorcist.*

Simon   Something like this happens . . .

Mark   It shits us up.

Simon   . . . What the fuck dae ye dae? Eh?

Johnny   What's wrong, Si? What's the fuckin score?

Simon   The gig's fucked. It's aw fuckin fucked!

Mark   He moans, in a high desperate whine. It was like a dug that hud been run ower and wis waiting fir some cunt tae pit it oot ay its misery.

Alison   The bairn's away! The bairn's away!!

Mark   We get up and go through tae the bedroom. Ah can feel death in the room before ah even see the bairn. It wis lyin face doon in its cot. It, naw, she, wis cauld n deid, blue aroond the eyes. Ah didnae huv tae touch her tae ken. Lyin thair like a wee doll at the bottom ay some kid's wardrobe.

Simon   That wee . . .

Johnny   So fuckin small.

Mark   Wee Dawn.

Johnny   Fuckin shame.

Simon   Wee Dawn.

Johnny   Fuckin sin man.

Mark   Ah'm fuckin right ootay here, man. Ah cannae fuckin handle this −

Simon   Nae cunt's leavin here the now!

Johnny   Stay cool, man. Stay cool . . .

Simon   Wuv goat fuckin gear stashed here. This street's been crawlin wi the fuckin DS for weeks now. We fucking charge oaf now, we aw fucking go doon. Thir's polis bastards every fucking where ootside.

Johnny   Aye, aye, but mibbe we should aw git the fuck ootay here, n Alison can git the ambulance or polis once wuv tidied up and fucked oaf.

Mark   Mibbe wuv goat tae stick wi Alison, likesay.
Like, mates n that. Ken?

Johnny   The way ah see it is thit it's Alison's bairn, ken?
Mibbe if she looked eftir it right, it might not be deid. How
should we get involved?

Mark   Hate tae say it, bit Johnny's goat a point. Ah'm
starting tae hurt really bad. Ah jist want tae take a shoat and
fuck off.

Johnny   Whae gied her the bairn?

Mark   Jimmy McGilvary, wiz it no?

Simon   Shite it fuckin wis.

Johnny   Dinnae you play Mister-fuckin-innocent!

Mark   Eh?! Moan tae fuck! Whit you oan about?

Johnny   You wir thair . . . Boab Sullivan's perty.

Mark   Naw, man, ah've nivir been wi Alison.

Johnny   How come ye wir crashed oot wi her in the mornin
at Sully's perty?

Mark   Ah wis fucked, man. Ootay ma box. Ah couldnae
huv goat a stiff nek wi a doorstep as a pillay.

Simon   Naw . . .

Mark   Ah cannae remember the last time ah hud a ride.

Simon   Naw . . .

Mark   Sick Boy puts a hand oan the deid bairn's cauld
cheek. Under the shades, tears fill his eyes.

Simon   Ah'm nivir touchin that shite again. Ah'm clean
fae now oan.

Johnny   C'moan, Si. Dinnae jump tae the wrong
conclusions. Whit happened tae the bairn's nowt tae dae wi
the skag. Ach, it's no Alison's fault either. She loved the
bairn. Snaebody's fault. Cot death. Ken? Happens aw the
time.

Mark   Yeah, likesay, cot death man . . .
Ah feel thit ah love thum aw. Ah want tae tell thum.
Ah try . . . but it comes oot as . . . 'Ah'm cookin'.

Simon   Fuck. (*Exits.*)

Johnny   Si! (*Exits.*)

Mark   That's me. Ah go ben the livin-room. Alison's nivir
moved. Ah feel thit ah should mibbe go and comfort her, pit
my airm aroond her. But ma bones feel twisted and scraped.
Ah couldnae touch anybody right now. Instead ah babble.
'Really sorry, Ali. Naebody's fault though. Cot death n that.
Wee Dawn. Barry wee bairn. Fuckin shame. Fuckin sin man,
ah'm tellin ye.' (Alison lifts her heid up an looks at us. Her
thin white face is like a skull wrapped in milky clingfilm; her
eyes are rid raw, circled wi black rings.)

Alison   Ye cookin, Mark? Ah need a shot. Ah really need a
fuckin shot. C'moan Marky, cook us up a shot.

We hear the distant echoing voices of children at play . . .

Alison *exits*.

7

Mark   Ten tins ay Heinz tomato soup. Eight tins ay
mushroom soup. All tae be consumed cold. One large tub ay
vanilla ice-cream – which will melt and be drunk. Two
boatils ay Milk of Magnesia, one boatil ay paracetamol, one
packet ay Rinstead mouth pastilles, one boatil ay
multivitamins, five litres ay mineral water, twelve Lucozade
isotonic drinks. And some magazines: soft porn, *Viz*, *Scottish
Football Today*, *The Punter*, etc. The most important item hus
already been procured from a visit tae the parental home . . .
Ma Ma's bottle ay valium, removed from her bathroom
cabinet. Ah don't feel bad about this. She never uses them
now. And if she does need them, her radge GP will prescribe
them like jelly tots. It's going tae be a hard week. Ma room is
bare and uncarpeted. There's a mattress in the middle ay the
flair with a sleeping bag oan it, an electric fire and a telly.
Ah've goat three brown plastic buckets wi a mixture ay

disinfectant and water – one for ma pish, one for ma shite and one for ma puke. You've got tae know what it's like tae try comin off the skag before ye can actually dae it. You can only learn through failure, and what ye learn is the importance ay preparation.

It starts as it generally does, with a slight nausea in the pit ay ma stomach and an irrational panic attack. As soon as ah become aware ay the sickness gripping me, it effortlessly moves from the uncomfortable tae the unbearable. A toothache starts tae spread fae ma teeth intae ma jaws and ma eye sockets. And then the sweat arrives . . . and then the shivers, covering ma back like a thin layer ay frost oan a car roof. It's time for action. No way can ah crash oot n face the music yet. Ah need . . . ah need . . . Ah need!

In twenty minutes ah wis in Muirhouse. Oan the bus an auld boot gies us the evil eye. No doubt ah'm fuckin boggin n looking a real mess. Doesnae bother us. A lassie sits across fae us listening tae her Walkman. Is she good looking? Whae cares? She's listenin tae Bowie – 'Golden Years'. Ah've goat every album Bowie ever made. The fuckin lot. Ah dinnae gie a fuck aboot him or his music. Ah only care aboot one thing. Some auld cunt is fartin and shitein at the driver aboot bus numbers and routes and times. Get the fuck oan or fuck off n die ya foostie auld cunt. Ah almost choked in rage at her selfish pettiness and the bus driver's pathetic indulgence of the cunt. When she finally gits oan the auld fucker has the cheek tae have a gob oan her like a cat's erse.

Ah'm gaunnae miss ma stoap! No. Ah get oaf at the shopping centre, the steel-shuttered units which huv nivir been let and the car park where cars huv nivir been parked fae twenty years. Ah slide along the wall. Ma guts are starting tae go: ah feel a queasy shifting in ma constipation. Ah arrive at the skag-merchant's door. He'll see ah'm suffering, and he'll gie us crap, cause the cunt knows ah'd walk oan ma hands and knees through broken gless tae use his shite fir toothpaste. But ah still love him. Ah huv tae. He's the boy holdin. He's holdin. Ah pull oot some crumpled notes fae ma poackits and flatten them oot oan the coffee table. He snaffles them and produces two wee hard bomb-shaped things wi a waxy coat oan them. Ah'd nivir seen the likes ay them before. 'What the fuck's this shite?!'

'Opium. Opium suppositories.'

'What the fuck dae ah dae wi these?'

'Dae ye really want me to tell ye? They melt through yir system, take away the pain, help ye git oaf the junk, right? That's the cunts they use in hoaspitals fir fucksakes.'

So . . . ah excuse masel, retire tae the toilet and insert them up ma erse. As ah leave he sais tae me, 'It'll take time,' and ah sais, 'You're tellin me: fir aw the good they've done so far ah might as well huv stuck thum up ma erse.'

But by the time ah hit the bottom ay the stair ah'm feeling better. The ache in ma body doesnae bother us. It feels like ah'm meltin inside. Ah huvnae shat fir aboot five or six days. As ah pass through the shopping centre ah fart. Fuck . . . Ah huv tae take immediate action.

There's a bookies in the shopping centre wi a toilet in the back. Ah dive in the smoke-filled shoap and head straight tae the bog. What a fuckin scene. Two guys standing in the doorway ay the toilet, just pishing intae the place which has a good inch ay stagnant urine covering the flair. Ah look across hopefully tae the cubicle. 'Bog's fuckin blocked, mate. Ye'll no be able tae shite in that,' sais one. Ah look sternly at him: 'Ah've goat tae fuckin go, mate. It looks fuckin awfay in thair, but it's either that or ma fuckin keks.' So . . . The bowl, the seatless bowl, is filled wi broon water n toilet paper n lumps ay floating shite. Ah whip oaf ma keks and sit on the cold wet porcelain shunky and ah empty ma guts: ma bowel, stomach, intestines, spleen, liver, kidneys, heart, lungs and fucking brains are aw falling through ma ersehole intae that bowl. Then ah realise what ah've done. Ah sit frozen fir a moment. But only a moment. Ah roll up ma shirt sleeves. There are scabby needlemarks along ma arms. But . . . ah plunge ma hands and forearms intae the broon water. Ah slosh around down there and get one ay ma bombs back straight away. Ah rub off some shite that's attached tae it. A wee bit melted but still largely intact. Ah stick it oan top ay the cistern. Locating the other takes several long dredges through the shite ay many good Muirhoose punters. Ah gag once, but eventually ah get ma lump ay white gold back, even better preserved than the first. Ma broon-stained airm reminds us ay the classic t-shirt tan: ah hud tae go right aroond the bend. Ah wis tempted tae swallay the suppositories, but ah rejected this notion almost as soon as it crossed ma mind. They were probably safer back where they came fae. Home they went. And home ah went.

It was a swelterin hot day. Ah remembered somebody hud said that it wis the first day ay the Edinburgh Festival. Certainly got the weather fir it. Back in ma room – ah couldnae face those three broon buckets.

8

Franco   Hoah! Marco! Yah smert cunt! Pit mah name doon fir the pool will ye, wuv a while before the train. (*Exits.*)

Mark   Ma first day at primary school, the teacher sais tae us 'You will sit beside Francis Begbie'. It wis the same story at secondary. Ah only did well at school tae get intae an O level class tae git away fae Begbie.

Franco (*returns with beers*)   Anywey the other fuckin week thair ah wis doon the fucking Volley wi Tommy n Rab and this cunt Jakey comes intae the pub. Ah minded ay the cunt, fuckin sure n ah did. Ah used tae think he wis a fuckin hard cunt back it the fuckin school, ken? Ah mind ay smashin loads ay fuckin crabs tae bits wi stanes wi that cunt doon the fuckin harbour, ken? He nivir recognised us. Didnae fuckin ken us fae Adam, the cunt. Anywey the cunt's mate, this fuckin plukey-faced wide-o, goes tae pit his fuckin money doon fir the baws it the table. Fir the pool, ken? Ah saes tae um 'That cunt's fuckin next mate,' pointin tae this wee specky gadge. This wee cunt's goat his fuckin name up oan the board, but he wid've jist fuckin sat thair n said fuck all if ah hudnae fuckin spoke like.

Ah wis fuckin game fir a swedge. If the cunts hud've fuckin come ahead it wis nae problem like. Ah mean, you ken me, ah'm no the type ay cunt thit goes lookin fir fuckin bothir likes, but ah wis the cunt wi the fuckin pool cue in ma hand, n

the plukey cunt could have the fat end ay it in his pus if he
wanted, like. Obviously ah wis cairryin ma fuckin chib n aw.
Too fucking right. Like ah sais ah dinnae go lookin fir fuckin
bother but if any lippy cunt wants tae start, ah'm fuckin
game. So the wee specky cunt's pit his fuckin dough in, n he's
rackin up n that, ken? The plukey cunt jist sits doon n says
fuck all. Ah kept ma eye oan the hard cunt, or at least he wis a
fuckin hard cunt it the school, ken. The cunt nivir sais a
fuckin wurd. Kept his fuckin mooth shut awright; the cunt.
Tommy says tae us, 'Hi Franco is that boy gettin lippy?' Ye
ken Tam, he's no fuckin shy, that cunt. They fuckin heard
um like, these cunts, but they nivir fuckin sais nowt again.
The plukey cunt and the so-called hard cunt. N it wid've
been two against two, cause you ken Rab; dinnae get us
wrong, ah lap the cunt up, but he's fuckin scoobied whin it
comes tae a pagger. He's pished ootay his fuckin heid n he kin
hardly haud the fuckin pool cue. This is fuckin half-past
eleven oan a Wednesday mornin wir talking aboot here. So it
wid've been fuckin square-gos. But they cunts sais fuck all.
Ah nivir fuckin rated the plukey cunt, but ah wis fuckin
disappointed in the hard cunt, or the so-called hard cunt,
like. He wisnae a fuckin hard man. A fuckin shitein cunt if the
truth be telt, ken. Big fucking disappointment tae me, the
cunt, ah kin tell ye.

Mark   Begbie is a cunt ay the first order, nae doubt about
that. The big problem is, he's a mate an aw. Ye cannae really
relax in his company, specially if he's hud a bevvy. Yir status
could change suddenly fae great mate intae persecuted
victim. So we indulge the radge, tell him he's the big man,
laugh at his murderous jokes. Ye know how it goes: ye laugh
with the rest o the cunts because ye'are feart no to, ye'are
feart tae stand oot fae the crowd; ye'are just a wee fucken
coward.
Ah mind the time me and Begbie wir lyin in the Links at the
bottom ay the running track. We were lyin doon there so's
we could see the lassies race in their wee shorts n blouses. We
were lying oan oor stomachs, heids propped up oan elbays n

hands, watching Lizzie MacIntosh pitting up a game race against the lanky strides ay big Morag –

Both 'Jam Rag!!!'

Mark – Henderson. Anywey ah hears this heavy breathin and turns tae notice Begbie slowly swivelling his hips, starin at the lassies, gaun –

Franco That wee Lizzie MacIntosh . . . total wee ride . . . fuckin shag the erse ofay that any day ay the week . . . the fuckin erse oan it . . . the fuckin tits oan it . . .

Mark Then he goes aw rigid and his erse is twitchin and his face faws doon intae the grass. Ah reach oot and pull Begbie ower oantay his back, exposing his knob which is drippin wi spunk and dirty wi earth. The cunt had slyly dug a hole in the turf wi his flick knife, and hud been fuckin the field. 'Ya dirty cunt, Franco!' Begbie jist pits his knob away, zips up, and graps a handful ay spunk n earth and –

Franco *rubs it in* **Mark***'s face. Confrontation.*

Mark (*backing down*) What kin ye dae? Ken, friendship wi Begbie is an ideal preparation for relating tae women. Ye learn sensitivity tae th'ither person's changing needs.

Franco Wummen!

Mark Cannae live wi em, cannae live withoot em.

9

Franco See ma heid was fuckin nippin this morning, ah kin fuckin tell ye. There's two boatils ay Becks in the fridge an ah down the cunts in double quick time an ah feel better right awey. Ah go back ben the bedroom and she's still fuckin sleeping . . .

Mark June?

Franco Lazy fat cunt. Jist cause she's huvin a fuckin bairn, thinks it gies her the right tae lie aroond aw fuckin day. Ah've goat tae pack a bag an ah'm lookin fir ma fuckin jeans and she's jist waking up.

June   Frank!

Franco   That cunt hud better huv washed ma fuckin 501s.

June   Frank, what are ye daein? Whair ur ye goan?

Franco   Ah'm ootay here. Whair the fuck's they soacks? Everythin takes twice as fuckin long whin yir hungower —

June   Whair ur ye goan?

Franco   N ah kin do withoot this cunt nippin ma fuckin heid.

June   Whair?

Franco   Ah telt ye, ah've goat tae fuckin nash. Ah pulled a bit ay business oaf n ah'm disappearing fir a couple ay weeks. Any polis cunts come tae the door, yuv no seen us fir yonks. Ye think ah'm oan the fuckin rigs, right? Yuv no seen us, mind.

June   But whair ur ye gaun Frank? Whair ur ye fuckin well gaun?

Franco   That's fir me tae ken n you tae find oot. What ye dinnae fuckin well ken they cannae fuckin well beat oot ay ye.

June   Ye cannae jist fuckin go like that!!!

Franco *kicks her*.

Franco   Nae cunt talks tae us like that. That's the fuckin rules ay the game, take it or fuckin leave it.

June   The bairn! Uh! The bairn!

Franco   The bairn!! The bairn!! Shut yir fuckin mooth aboot the fuckin bairn! It's probably no even mah fuckin bairn anywey. Shavin gear . . .

June   Get the doaktir.

Franco   Ah'm fuckin late, ah've nae time. S'yir fault. See if ah'm fuckin late fir thit train —

June   Ah hurt, ah hurt . . . Get the doaktir . . .

Franco Goat tae fuckin nash.

June The bairn . . .

Franco Ah've hud bairns before, wi other lassies. Ah ken whit it's aw aboot. She thinks it's aw gaunnae be fuckin great whin the bairn comes, but she's in fir a fuckin shock. Ah kin tell ye aw aboot fuckin bairns. Pain in the fuckin erse.

June Fraaaank!!

Franco 'Time fir a sharp exit'.
Hoah! Marco! Yah smert cunt! Pit mah name doon fir the pool will ye, wuv goat a while before the train. (*Exits.*)

10

Tommy Did ye see that? Pure fuckin mental. Ah'm sittin in the bar there wi Davie Mitchell ken, wir likesay oot fir a quick drink. N this boy is huvin words wi a lassie he's with:

Boy Cause ah fuckin sais! That's fuckin how!

Tommy N he hits her.

Boy *hits* **Lassie**.

Tommy No a fuckin slap or nowt like that, but a punch. Naebody bothers. A big punter at the bar wi long blond corkscrew hair n a rid coupon looks ower n smiles, then turns back tae watch the darts match. No one ay the boys playin darts turns roond. Whin ah git tae the bar tae get us a couplay pints in, thuv started again. Ah kin hear thum.

Lassie Gaun then. Dae it again. Gaun then!

Boy *hits* **Lassie**.

Tommy Blood spurts fae her mooth.

Lassie Hit us again, fuckin big man. Gaun then!

Boy *hits* **Lassie**.

Tommy She lets oot a scream, then starts greetin. The corkscrew-heided cunt catches ma eye n smiles. 'Lovers' tiff,' he sais. Ah look ower tae the barman, an auld guy wi grey hair n a moustache. He shakes his heid and sais 'They should be daein that kind ay arguin in the hoose, no in a pub.' Nivir, ivir hit a lassie, ma faither often telt us. It's the lowest scum thit dae that son, he sais. This cunt thit's hittin this lassie fits the bill: he's goat greasy black hair, a thin white face n a black moustache. A wee ferret-faced fucker. Now, ah dinnae want tae be here. Ah jist came oot fir a quiet drink wi Davie. Only a couple, ah promised him, tae git um tae come. Ah've goat the bevvyin under control, jist pints like, nae nips, bit this kind ay thing makes us want a wee whisky. Lizzie's away tae her mother's. No comin back, she sais. Ah came fir a pint. The lassie's eye is swollen and shuttin. Her jaw's swollen n aw, and her mooth is still bleedin. She's a skinny lassie n she looks like she'd snap intae pieces if he hit her again. Still, she carries oan . . .

Lassie   That's yir answer. That's eywis yir answer.

Boy   Shut it! Ah'm tellin ye! Shut the fuck up!

Lassie   Whit ye gaunnae dae?

Boy   Ya fackin –

Tommy   Hoah! That's enough mate. Leave it. Yir ootay order.

Boy   It's nane ay your fuckin business! You keep ootay this!

Tommy   Ah'm makin it ma fuckin business. Whit you gaunnae fuckin dae aboot it?

Boy   You want yir mooth punched?

Tommy   Think ah'm gaunnay jist sit here n lit ye dae it? Fuckin wide-o! Oootside then cunt. Cumaun!

Lassie (*attacking* **Tommy**)   That's ma man! That's ma fackin man yir talkin tae! That's mah man . . .

11

Franco   Fucked if ah'm gaunnae stey wi that fuckin June eftir the bairn's here. Ivir since she's been huvin that bairn, she thinks she kin git fuckin lippy wi us.

Mark We'd better be movin. Wuv goat the cairry-oot tae organise. The London train'll be fuckin mobbed.

Franco Aye, right. Aw they cunts wi backpacks n luggage . . . n bairns' fuckin go-carts. Shouldnae huv bairns oan a fuckin train. What ye gittin?

Mark Boatil ay voddy n a few cans.

Franco Ah'm gittin a boatil ay J.D. n eight cans ay Export. Ah might git Lorraine tae fill up a couple ay draftpaks n aw.

Mark Thill be a couple ay draftpaks gittin well filled up oan the train gaun doon.

Franco If ah had ma fuckin wey, the train wouldnae stoap for aw they cunts thit've booked fae Berwick n aw they fuckin places; it wid jist be Edinburgh tae London that wid be it, enday fuckin story. Ah speak ma fuckin mind, whitivit any cunt sais. Aw they booked seats. Fuckin liberty, so it is. It should be first come, first fuckin served. Aw this bookin seats shite . . . ah'll gie the cunts bookin seats . . .
Nae cunt gets fuckin lippy wi me, bairn or nae fuckin bairn. She kens that, n she still gits fuckin smert. See if anything's happened tae that fuckin bairn . . . That cunt's deid if she's made us hurt that fuckin bairn.
That Lorraine's a wee fuckin ride. Ah've goat a feeling that she's goat the hots fir us, cause she ey goes that fuckin quiet, shy wey whin ah fuckin talk tae her. Once ah git back fae London ah'll fuckin move in thair, pretty fuckin sharpish n aw. Ya cunt. (*Exits.*)

12

Musical interlude. Maybe the girl skins up. Maybe **Mark** *shoots up. Maybe we see* **Lizzie** *walking out on* **Tommy**.

13

Tommy Ah split up wi Lizzy.

Mark Ye pished oaf aboot it?

Tommy   Dinnae ken. If ah'm honest, ah'll miss the sex maist. That n like, jist huvin somebody, ken? (*He wanders.*)

Mark   Lizzie MacIntosh. Ah telt ye the time me and Begbie wir lyin watching the lassies racin? Naw, doesnae matter.

Tommy (*seeing* **Mark**'s *works*)   What does it dae fir ye Mark?

Mark   Doan't start oan me. Ah ken ah'm killin maself n ah huv tae pack it in cause ah kin live ma life withoot it n aw that: ye've telt us before, Tam, jist like ma auld lady.

Tommy   Naw, tell us. Ah want tae ken.

Mark   Ah dinnae really know, Tam, ah jist dinnae. It kinday makes things seem mair real tae us. Life's boring and futile. We start oaf wi high hopes, then we bottle it. We realise that we're aw gaunnae die, without really findin oot the big answers. Basically, we live a short, disappointing life; and then we die. We fill up oor lives wi shite, things like careers and relationships tae delude oorselves that it isnae aw totally pointless. Smack's an honest drug, because it strips away these delusions. Wi smack, whin ye feel good, ye feel immortal. Whin ye feel bad, it intensifies the shite that's already thair. It's the only really honest drug. It doesnae alter your consciousness. It jist gies ye a hit and a sense ay well-being. Eftir that, ye see the misery ay the world as it is; ye cannae anaesthetise yirsel against it.

Tommy   Shite. Pure shite.

Mark   It's also a fuckin good kick.

Tommy   Gies a go. Gies a hit.

Mark   Fuck off, Tommy.

Tommy   Ye sais it's a good kick. Ah pure wantae try it.

Mark   Ye dinnae. C'moan Tommy, take ma word fir it.

Tommy   Ah've goat the hireys. C'moan. Cook us up a shot.

Mark Tommy . . . fuck sake man . . .

Tommy Ah'm tellin ye, cmoan. Supposed tae be fuckin
mates, ya cunt. Cook us up a shot. Ah kin fuckin handle it.
One fuckin shot isnae gaunnae hurt us. C'moan.

Alison 'Life's boring and futile. We start oaf wi high
hopes, then we bottle it. We realise that we're aw gaunnae
die, without really findin oot the big answers. Basically, we
live a short, disappointing life; and then we die. We fill up oor
lives wi shite, things like careers and relationships tae delude
oorselves that it isnae aw totally pointless. Smack's an honest
drug.' Shite. Poor shite.
He droaps a filter intae the spoon n blaws oan it, before
sucking up the smack through the needle intae the barrel ay
the syringe . . . He's goat a fuckin huge blue vein tapped up
. . . He pierces the flesh and injects a wee bit, slowly, before
sucking blood back intae the barrel. His lips are quivering as
he gazes pleadingly at him for a second or two and then he
fires the life-giving . . . life-taking . . .
Their eyes are innocent and full ay wonder, like a bairn's
thit's come through on Christmas morning tae a pile ay gift-
wrapped presents stacked under a tree. They baith look
strangely beautiful in the candlelight.

Mark Awright . . . ?

Tommy This is pure fucking brilliant Mark . . . ah'm
fuckin buzzin here . . . ah'm jist pure buzzin . . .

Mark See . . . some cunts are so . . . predisposed tae
smack.
Ah cleaned the fuckin needle!
See ma problem is, whenever ah sense the possibility, or
realise the actuality ay attaining something that ah thought
ah wanted, girlfriend, flat, joab, education, money, whitevir,
it jist seems sae dull n sterile that ah cannae value it any mair.
Junk's different though. Ye cannae turn yir back oan it sae
easy. It willnae let ye. Trying tae manage a junk problem is
the ultimate challenge. Ah mean . . . it's real.

Tommy *throws up*.

Mark   Yuv done it mate. That's you goat the set now. Dope, acid, speed, E, mushies, nembies, vallies, smack, the fucking lot. Knock it oan the heid. Make that the first n last time.

Tommy   Too fuckin right.

Mark   Split up wi Lizzie then?

Tommy   Ah just pure wish Lizzy wid eywis be like she is in bed.

Mark   Shag extraordinaire?

Tommy   Sweet and beautiful. Ah know ah shouldnae be tellin aboot it man, but . . . god . . . hur in bed . . . Ah'm addicted tae having sex wi her. God. Yellow silk pillowcases. They ones Davie gied us.

Mark   Ah wis with him when he knocked them off.

Tommy   Her hair on the pillow . . .

Mark   British Home Stores . . .

Tommy   Ah love daein it fae behind . . .

Mark   But she's kicked ye intae touch?

Tommy   Ah forgot her birthday. Ah mean ah goat ma ticket fir the Iggy Pop gig when ah goat ma giro n that wis me pure skint. Ah mean it wis the ticket or a birthday present fir Lizzie. Nae contest. Ah thought she'd understand. It's ma ain fault. Ah should've said nothing aboot the ticket. Ah get too excited . . . ah pure open ma big mooth far too wide.

Alison   'So. Ye'd rather go tae a concert wi Davie fuckin Mitchell than the pictures wi me?'

Mark   The rhetorical question!

Tommy   That's pure Lizzie.

Mark   The stock-in-trade weapon ay burds n psychos.

Tommy   She's goat this – outrage.

Mark   She's goat a tongue like a sailor.

Tommy   She calls me all the fuck-ups under the sun.

Alison   All the fuck-ups under the sun.

Mark   The pure viciousness ay hur expression –

Tommy   Ye can see her point.

Mark   – will corrode her beauty before its time . . .

Tommy   Ah'm jist auld fuck the wind.

Mark   . . . but her pretty head resting on the yellow silk pillowcase . . .

Tommy   Daein it fae behind . . .

Alison   Daein it fae behind . . .

Tommy   Ah loved her but.

Mark   Make that the first and last time.

Tommy   Too fuckin right.

Alison   Och, why don't they just fuck each other?

Tommy and **Mark** (*singing*)   'Love, love me do. You know –'

Alison   Mark says that love doesnae exist. Like god. But I've goat some White Doves.

Tommy   Eckeys!

Alison and **Tommy**   Excellent!

Mark   Maist Ecstasy hasnae goat any MDMA in it. It's just part speed part acid.

Alison   This gear is pure freaky but.

Tommy   Lurve!

Tommy and **Alison**   Lurve!

Mark   Love is like religion. The state wants ye tae believe in that kinday crap so's they kin control ye, n fuck yer heid up. Ach c'moan!

Alison   Let's float ootay here n cross over tae the Meadows.

Tommy   Aye, let's hit the Meadows. Thuv goat big theatre tent and a funfair.

Mark   Aye . . .

14

Music/effects. They wander through the funfair . . .

Alison   Ah like that. Ah really like that . . .

They go on a ride . . . Thrills! They wander through the Meadows . . .

Mark   Tam! There's a fuckin squirrel at yir feet.

Tommy   Aw, magic! Wee silvery thing . . .

Alison   C'moan . . .

Mark   Kill the cunt!

Tommy   Naw!

Mark   Goan!

Tommy   O fucksake man, leave it! Squirrel's botherin nae cunt!

Mark   Git a haud ay the cunt! Where the fuck did it go tae?

Alison   Naw, look, see, they wifies, they're lookin at ye! Mark, Tam, c'moan, see they posh wifies! I'm tellin ye! What the fuck are yes looking at? Ye want a fuckin picture doll?

Mark   C'moan, Tam, wrap it in cellophane so's it doesnae split whin ye fuck it!

Tommy   Naw, he's daein his ain thing!

Mark   Whae's the foostie-minged fucker starin at? Whit ye cruisin us fir ye tea-room hags? Ah'd rather stick it between a couple ay B&Q sandin blocks, doll!

Alison   Fahk aff! You'd shag the crack ay dawn if it hud hairs oan it!

Mark   Ah could shag a hairy donut the night!

Mark *chases* **Alison** *off . . . then returns.*

Mark   C'moan, Tam. Fucksakes, man, what is it?

Tommy   Youse wir gaunnae kill that squirrel.

Mark   'Sony a fuckin squirrel, Tam. Thir vermin.

Tommy   It's mibbe nae mair vermin thin you or me, likesay. Whae's tae say what's vermin? They posh wifies think people like us ur vermin, likesay, does that make it right thit they should kill us?

Mark   Sorry, Tommy. 'Sony a squirrel. Sorry mate. Ah ken how ye feel aboot animals . . .

Tommy   It's wrong man . . . Ye cannae love yirsel if ye want tae hurt things like that . . .

Mark   Ah jist, like, ye ken whit ah mean Tommy it's like . . .

Tommy   Ah mean . . . what hope is thir?

Mark   . . . fuck, ah'm fucked up, Tommy. Ah dinnae ken.

Tommy   The squirrel's likes fuckin lovely . . .

Mark   Aw the fightin . . . aw the gear . . . the drugs . . .

Tommy   . . . he's daein his ain thing . . . he's free.

Mark   Ah dinnae ken what ah'm daein wi ma life . . . it's aw jist a mess, Tommy. Ah dinnae ken whit the fuckin score is. Sorry man. Sorry. (*Hug.*) Yir one ay the best, man. Remember that. That's no the drink n the drugs talkin, that's me talkin.

Alison   Look at ma nipples . . . they feel fuckin weird . . . nae cunt's goat nipples like mine . . .

They compare nipples, ad lib. Then hug . . .

All (*loved up*)   Love, love me do . . .

Sudden loud music/effects . . .

Franco *erupts onto the scene, bloodied, chib-waving . . .*

Franco (*to assailants off*)   Cummoan ya cunts cummoan this is the fuckin Beggar! Cummoan!

Tommy *accidentally gets slashed.*

Alison   Tommy!

All run off.

Part Two

15

Flag-draped coffin.

Newscaster   Another soldier has been shot and killed in
Northern Ireland. Lance Corporal William Renton of the
Royal Scots Dragoon Guards was 27. He came from Leith in
Edinburgh. The Northern Ireland Secretary condemned the
killing as a loathsome and cowardly act. This brings the total
number of deaths associated with terrorism in Northern
Ireland this year to 42. The Economy: the markets closed
today at an all-time high, the FTSE . . .

Mark   Billy Boy. Billy Boy. Ah remember you sittin oan
top ay us. Me helplessly pinned tae the flair. Windpipe
constricted tae the width ay a straw. Praying, as the oxygen
drained fae ma lungs and brain, that Ma would return fae
Presto's before you crushed the life oot ay ma skinny body.
The smell ay pish fae your genitals – the damp patch oan yer
short troosers. Was it that exciting, Billy? Ah hope so. Ah
cannae really grudge ye it now. Ye always had a problem
that way; sudden discharges of faeces and urine that used tae
drive Ma tae distraction. So on patrol in Crossmaglen, ye left
your armoured car tae examine a road block. Then pow!
zap! bang! and ye were deid. 'He died a hero' they say. In
fact he died a spare prick in a uniform, walkin along a
country road wi his rifle in his hand, an ignorant tool ay
imperialism. That was the biggest crime: you understood
fuck all aboot it. You died as you lived: completely fuckin
scoobied. You made the *News at Ten*, but. Three minutes ay
fame, like a fuckin advert. And some ruling-class cunt, a
minister ay some description, says in his cut-glass accent how
you were 'a brave young man', and your murderers will be
'ruthlessly hunted down'. And so they fuckin should be. All
the wey tae the Houses ay Parliament.
Ken whit the daft cunt turns roond n sais tae us?
Dinnae matter.

It's weird standin round a grave. Davie's here somewhere. Jist outay prison. Tommy n aw. Tommy's lookin like death. Ma cousin Nina looks intensely shaftable. She's goat long dark hair blowing in the wind and is wearing an ankle-length black coat. Seems tae be a bit ay a Goth. Ah give her a broad wink and she smiles, embarrassed. Ma faither's been clocking this and he steams ower tae me: 'Wahn fuckin bit ay crap oot ay you n that's us finished. Right?' His eyes were tired, sunk deep intae their sockets. There was a sad unsettling vulnerability about him ah'd nivir seen before. Ah wanted tae say so much tae the man, but resented him fir allowing this circus tae take place. 'Leave it to us,' the softly-spoken Army Welfare Officer told Ma. Leave it to us . . . Ah seethed when ah saw that fuckin Union Jack oan his coffin. One ay his squaddy mates sidles up tae me. 'You were 'is bruvver,' he sais, choppers hingin oot tae dry. Every cunt's eyes focus oan us. 'Billy n me nivir agreed oan that much,' ah sais, 'but one thing we hud in common wis thit we both liked a good bevvy and a good crack. If he can see us now, he'll be laughin his heid oaf at us standin here aw moosey faced. He'd be sayin 'Enjoy yirsels, fir god sake!' Ay, stick tae the cliches. It's the best way tae strike a chord without compromising too much wi the sickenin hypocrisy which fills the room. Decency! Ah gie thum all a beery grin. But ma Uncle Charlie sees through ma game.

'Listen son, if you don't get oan yir fuckin bike, ah'm gaunnae tan your jaw. If it wisnae fir yir faither thair, ah've done it a long time ago. Yir brother wis ten times the man you'll evir be, ya fucking junky. If you knew the misery yuv caused yir Ma n Da.'

'You can speak frankly,' ah cut in.

'Oh, ah'll speak frankly aw right, ye smert cunt. Ah'll knock ye through that fuckin waw.'

His chunky indian-inked fist was just a few inches fae ma face. Ma grip tensed oan the whisky gless ah wis haudin. If he moved he wis gittin this gless. 'If ye did gie us a kickin,' ah sais, 'ye'd be daein us a favour. Ah'd jist huv a wank aboot it later on. We drop-oot university junkies are kinky that wey. Cause that's aw you're worth, ya fuckin trash. Ye want tae

go ootside, just say the fuckin word.' The room seemed tae
shrink tae the size ay Billy's coffin. The cunt pushed us gently
in the chest.
'Wuv had wahn funeral in the family the day, wir no wantin
another.'
Good story . . . good story. Ah went through tae the toilet.
Ah went through tae the toilet, Billy. Ur ye listenin? Sharon
wis comin out. Sharon n me huv mibbe spoken about half a
dozen sentences tae each other, ivir. Her face was flushed n
bloated wi alcohol n pregnancy. Ah sais tae her, 'You n me
need tae huv a wee blether likes.' N ah usher her intae the
toilet n loak the door behind us. Ah start tae feel her up . . .
while rabbitin a load of shite aboot how we huv tae stick
thegither at a time like this. Ah'm feelin her lump n gaun oan
aboot how much responsibility ah felt taewards ma unborn
niece or nephew. We start kissin, and ah move ma hand
doon, feelin the panty lines through the cotton material ay
her maternity dress. Ah wis soon fingerin her fanny, and she
hud goat ma prick oot ay ma troosers. Ah wis still bullshittin,
tellin her that ah'd always admired her as a person and a
woman, which she disnae really need tae hear because she's
gaun doon oan us, bit it's somehow comfortin tae say. She
gies a good blowjob. N ah wis thinkin, if only Billy could see
us now. It wis the first good thoughts aboot ye ah'd hud,
y'cunt. Ah withdraw, jist before comin, and guide Sharon
intae the doggy position. Ah love daein it fae behind. She has
a powerful ivy smell. It's a wee bit like throwing the
proverbial sausage up a close, but ah find ma stroke and she
tightens up. They say that a shag is good for an unborn child,
circulation of blood or that. Ah can see masel, stickin it – A
knock oan the door. Auntie Effie's high nasal voice.
'Whit ye daein in thair?'
'Sawright, Sharon's bein sick. Too much bevvy in her
condition.'
'Ur you seein tae her, son?'
'Aye . . . ah'm seein tae hur.'
'Awright well.'
Ah blurt oot ma muck n pull oot. Ah gently push hur
prostrate, helping her turn ower, and scoop her huge milky

tits oot ay her dress. Ah snuggle intae them like a bairn. She starts strokin ma heid. Ah feel wonderful, so at peace.

'That wis fuckin barry.'

'Will we keep seein each other now, eh?'

What a fuckin radge. 'Wuv tae git up, Sharon, git cleaned, likes, ken. They widnae understand if they caught us. Ah know that yir a good lassie, Sharon, but they dinnae understand fuck all.'

'Ah ken you're a nice laddie.' She was caught in this git-a-man git-a-bairn git-a-hoose shite that lassies get drummed intae them; mashed tattie fir brains. Ah took her back tae ma flat. We jist talked. She telt us a load ay things thit ah wanted tae hear, things ma Ma n faither never knew, and wid hate tae know. How you were a cunt tae her, Billy. How ye battered her, humiliated her, and generally treated her like a piece of shite. 'Whit did ye stey wi um fir?' ah asked. And she sais . . . she sais, 'He wis ma felly. Ye eywis think it'll be different, thit ye kin change thum, thit ye kin make a difference.' Aw Billy. (*He kicks the coffin; it collapses into planks and chairs.*)

Music: 'Amazing Grace'.

Mark   Aw fucksakes! Billy! Ah didnae –
(*Frantically injecting.*) 'If ye did gie us a kickin, ye'd be daein us a favour. Ah'd jist huv a wank aboot it later on. We drop-oot junkies are kinky that wey. Cause that's aw you're worth, ya fuckin trash. Ye want tae go ootside, just say the fuckin word.' The room seemed tae shrink tae the size ay Billy's coffin. 'Wuv had wahn funeral in the family the day, wir no wa–'. Ah! Ah! Fu– fu–

Lights fail to momentary blackout as **Mark** *gets to a chair.*

Mother   Ah'll help ye, son. Ah'll help ye fight this disease. (*Tucks duvet round* **Mark**.) Ah've loast one laddie already, ah'm no losin another yin! Ye'll stay here wi me n yir faither until yir better. Wir gaunnae beat this son, wir gaunnae beat it. (*Switches off radio.*) They played that at the funeral. 'Amazing Grace'. (*Exits.*)

Mark   Ma heid struggles tae piece thegither how ah've goat here. Ah can remember Johnny Swan's place, then feeling like ah wis gaunnae die. Then Johnny and Alison takin us doon the stairs, gittin us intae a taxi n bombin up tae the Infirmary. Overdose. Takes yer breath away. Ye try tae take a breath and it feels as if a thin stream ay air is coming intae yir boady fae a bullet hole in yir back. Then they shut the hole. He must've given thum ma Ma's address. N here ah am. In the junky's limbo, too sick tae sleep, too tired tae stay awake. A twilight zone where nothing's real. 'Ah'll help ye, son . . . Wir gaunnae beat this disease . . .'

Mother (*bringing tray*)   Ye'll git through it though son. Doctor Mathews sais it's jist really like a bad flu. (*Exits.*)

Mark   When wis the last time auld Mathews hud cauld turkey? Ah'd like tae lock that dangerous auld radge in a padded cell fir a fortnight, and gie um a couple ay injections ay diamorphine a day, then leave the cunt fir a few days. He'd be beggin us fir it eftir that. Ah'd jist shake ma heid and say 'Take it easy, mate. What's the fuckin problem? It's jist like a bad flu.' Did he gie us temazepam?

Mother (*brings ketchup*)   Naw! Ah telt um, nane ay that rubbish. Ye wir worse comin oaf that thin ye wir wi heroin. Ye wir in a hell ay a state. Nae mair drugs.

Mark   Mibbe ah could go back tae the clinic, Ma?

Mother   Naw! Nae clinics. Nae methadone. That made ye worse, son, ye said so yirself. Ye lied tae us, son. Tae yir ain mother n faither. Ye took that methadone n still went oot scorin. Fae now oan son, it's a clean brek. Yir stayin here whair ah kin keep an eye oan ye. Ah've loast one laddie already. Ah'm no losin another yin! (*Brings food.*)

Mark   Ah've telt ye ah dinnae eat meat, Ma.

Mother   Ye eywis liked yir mince n totties. That's whair ye've gone wrong son, no eating the right things. Ye need meat. It's good steak mince. (*With a forkful of mince.*) Come on son, make a tunnel for the choo-choo . . . remember?

Mark   No Mummy no!

He takes a fit and blacks out.
Nightmare effects. Train noise. **Mother** *transforms into* **Franco**.

Franco (*screaming-pitch*)   If ah had ma *fuckin* wey, the train
wouldnae stoap for aw they *cunts* thit've booked fae Berwick
n aw they *fuckin* places; it wid jist be Edinburgh tae London
that wid be it, end ay *fuckin* story!!!
Oan the train, Mark sits doon beside two burds. Fuckin tidy
n aw. Good fuckin choice. 'These seats are free until
Darlington,' he sais. Ah grabs the reservation cairds n sticks
thum in ma tail – 'Thir fuckin free the whole wey doon now.
Ah'll gie the cunts bookin,' ah sais, smilin at one ay the burds.
Too fuckin right n aw. Forty quid a ticket. No shy they
British Rail cunts, ah kin fuckin tell ye.
He's tannin the voddy. Well, if thats the wey the cunt wants
tae fuckin play it, ah grabs the J.D. n swigs it back. 'Here we
go, here we go, here we go,' ah sais. That cunt jist smiles. He
keeps lookin ower it the burds, thir likesay American, ken.
Problem wi that smert cunt is thit he's no goat the gift ay the
gab is far as burds go, likes. No likesay me n Sick Boy. He jist
cannae really fuckin relate tae burds. Ye wait oan that cunt
tae make the first fuckin move, ye'll be waitin a long fuckin
time. Ah fuckin show the smert cunt how it's done. 'No
fuckin shy, they British Rail cunts, eh?' ah sais, nudgin the
burd next tae us. 'Whair's it yis come fae then?'

He is trying to get **Mark** *to respond.*

These foreign cunts've goat trouble wi the Queen's fuckin
English, ken. Ye huv tae speak louder, slower, n mair posh
likes. 'WHERE . . . DAE . . . YEZ . . . COME . . . FAE?'
'Tirawnto. That wis the Lone Ranger's mate, wis it no?' The
burds jist look it us. Some punters dinnae understand the
Scottish sense ay humour.
'Where are you from?' the other burd asks. Pair ay rides n
aw. The smert cunt made a good fuckin move sittin here, ah
kin tell ye. And then Mark sais, you sais, cummoan ya cunt,
you fucking sais, she sais Where do you come from? and you
sais –

Mark (*sitting up*)   'Edinburgh'.

Franco (*moved*)   Smarmy cunt. Aw ready tae steam in now once Franco breks the fuckin ice! 'Edinburgh'!
These burds are gaun oantay us aboot how fuckin beautiful Edinburgh is, and how lovely the fuckin castle is oan the hill ower the gairdins n aw that shite. That's aw they tourist cunts ken though, the castle n Princes Street, n the High Street. Like whin Monny's auntie came ower fae that wee village oan that island oaf the west coast ay Ireland, wi aw her bairns. The wifey goes up tae the council fir a hoose. The council sais tae her, whair's it ye want tae fuckin stey, like? The woman sais, ah want a hoose in Princes Street lookin oantay the castle. This wifey's fuckin scoobied likes, speaks the fuckin Gaelic is a first language, disnae even ken that much English. Perr cunt jist liked the look ay the street whin she came oaf the train, thoat the whole fuckin place wis like that. The cunts it the council jist laugh n stick the cunt in one ay they hoatline joabs in West Granton, thit nae cunt else wants. Instead ay a view ay the castle, she's goat a view ay the gasworks. That's how it fuckin works in real life, if ye urnae a rich cunt wi a big fuckin hoose n plenty poppy. Real life uh?

Mark   Oh to, oh to be, oh to be a Hi-bee. Oh to, oh to be, oh to be a Hi-bee. Oh to –

Both   – oh to be, oh to be a Hi-bee. Oh to, oh to be, oh to be a Hi-bee! (*Leave together.*)

17

Bar music in the background. **Alison** *clears up* . . .

Alison   Ah'm workin in a restaurant bar. It's one o they quiet nights. Graham's in the kitchen preparing food that he hopes somebody will eat. Four guys come intae the restaurant. Obviously drunk. They sit doon at a table n order. 'A couple of bottles of your best piss.' English settlers. Ah smile at them, though. Ye huv tae learn tae treat people as people. One sais tae another: 'What do you call a good-looking girl in Scotland?' The other sais: 'A tourist!' Then one sais, gesturing in ma direction: 'I don't know though. I wouldn't kick that out of bed!' Doss prick. Ah cannae afford tae lose this joab. Ah need the money. 'Oroit darlin?' he sais, studying the menu: dark-haired skinny wanker wi a long fringe. 'Orroit?' Ah dinnae need this shite. Takin the order is a nightmare. They're engrossed in conversation aboot careers, computers, marketing, life in the fast lane . . . in between trying tae humiliate me. The skinny wanker actually asks us whit time ah finish, n the rest make whooping noises and dae drum rolls on the table. D'ye understand how ah feel? Debased. Whin ah get in the kitchen ah'm shakin wi rage. 'Can ye no git these fuckin arseholes ootay here?' ah sais tae Graham. 'Business,' he says. 'The customer ma dear is always right, even if he is a knob-end.' Ah wish thit Louise or Marisa was on thenight, another woman tae talk tae. Ah'm smack-bang in the middle ay a heavy period n ah'm feelin that scraped out n drained wey. Ah go tae the toilet n change tampons, wrapping the used one up in some toilet paper. A couple of thum's ordered tomato and orange soup. Trendy. Graham's busy preparing the main courses, so ah take the bloodied tampon and lower it intae the first bowl ay soup. Like a tea-bag. Ah squeeze it with a fork. A couplay strands ay black uteral lining float in the soup, before being dissolved wi a healthy stir. Ah deliver the two pate starters and two tomato n orange soups tae the table, making sure that the skinny gelled-up fuck-wit has goat the spiked one. 'More wine!' the fat, fair-heided prick petulantly booms at us. They're talking about how terribly hoat it is in Hawaii, makes ye sweat like a pig. 'More wine!' Ah go back tae the lavvy and fill a saucepan wi urine. Ma urine has that stagnant, cloudy look which suggests a urinary tract infection. Cystitis? Ah add some tae the carafe ay wine. Looks a bit cloudy but they're so smashed they winnae notice. Ah pour some more ay ma pish ontae the fish. It's a – fennel sauce, ah think. 'S a fanny sauce the now. They pricks eat and drink everything withoot even noticing! It's hard tae shite ontae a piece of paper. 'Sonly a wee lavvy. Ah manage a small runny turd which ah take through and whizz up wi some cream in the liquidiser and then merge wi the chocolate

sauce heating away in the pan. Profiteroles. Profiteroles all round! It's a loat easier tae keep smilin now. Ah feel charged wi a great power. The fat bastard hus drawn the really short straw. His ice-cream is laced wi ground up traces ay rat poison. No, ground up traces of broken glass . . . No . . . Too radge . . . It's all too mad . . .
What planet are we oan?

18

Music . . . rain . . .

Tommy Laura McEwan. Lorra McEwaaan! Sounds barry likesay. 'Ah don't want ye tae hurt me . . . the minute ah start tae feel pain it's fuckin over'. Oooh! Aaah . . . Ah nivir did get Laura –
Ah split up wi Lizzie!

Alison It is 5.06 a.m. and the pub's yellow lights fall on the dark wet lifeless street.

Franco . . . so ah'm oan toap ay this burd, ken, cowpin it likes, gaun fuckin radge, n it's fuckin screamin likes n ah thinks fuck me this dirty cow's right intae it likes –

Tommy Fuckin weird, man . . .

Franco Fuck off! Fuckin junky . . .

Mark Tam? Tam! How ye daein man?

Tommy Fuckin weird . . . you n me . . .

Mark Whit ye drinkin?

Tommy Naw . . . Goat any smack?

Mark Fucksake, Tommy. Forget it man. Leave it alane while ye still can.

Tommy Ah can handle it. Are ye cairryin?

Mark Ah'm clean.

Tommy Aw . . .

Mark *gives him some money.* **Tommy** *hurries off.*

Franco   'Kin junkie!
Anywey ah thinks fuck me this dirty cow's right intae it likes,
but it pushes us oaf, ken n she's bleedin ootay her fanny ken,
like it's fuckin rag week, n ah'm aboot tae say, that disnae
bother me, specially no wi a fuckin root oan like ah hud,
ah'm fuckin tellin ye. Anywey, it turns oot thit the cunt is
huvin a fuckin miscarriage thair n then!
Is that no funny?
(*Sings.*) 'Those were the days my friend, we thought they'd
never end.'

Mark   How's June?

Franco   Who?

Alison   'How's June,' he said, 'how's June?' Remember?
'Who?' End of conversation.

Franco   How's Alison?

Mark   Wee Dawn, wee Dawn . . . Fucking shame, cot
death . . .

Franco   Ach, the wee lassie wid huv died ay fuckin AIDS if
it hudnae died ay coat death. Easier fuckin death fir a bairn.

Mark   She didnae huv HIV!

Franco   Whae's tae say?

Mark   Nae cunt really kens . . .

Alison   Ye can lose them at any time. Before they're even
born. Even eftir thir born, ye can lose them. Ma Auntie
Jeannie says thit eftir they're seven you lose them. Then just
whin ye think ye've adjusted, it happens again when they're
fourteen. And then the heroin. 'Ah'll help ye son, ah'll help
ye fight this disease. Wir gaunnae beat it, son, wir gaunnae
beat it.' But the bairn's away, the bairn's away.

Tommy *enters naked, with a candle.*

Alison   O! O son . . . ! O son . . .

Tommy *cooks up.*

Alison   Hail Mary full of grace, the Lord is with thee,
blessed art thou among women and blessed is the fruit of thy
womb, Jesus. Holy Mary, Mother of God, pray for us sinners
now and in the hour of our death . . .

Tommy *injects into his penis.*

Alison   Nawww!

Tommy *collapses.*

Alison   Mark. Ye smert cunt. Ken thit Tommy's sick?!

Mark   Aye. Ah heard.

Alison   Go n fuckin see the cunt. Go n fuckin see the cunt.

Mark   How ye feelin?

Tommy   No bad. Cold but.

Mark (*puts his coat round his shoulders*)   Yir lookin well.

Tommy   Ah'm gaunnae die.

Mark   Some time in the next fifteen years. Ye can step out
in the street under a fuckin bus.
Want tae talk aboot it?

Tommy   No really. See whit they painted oan ma door?

Mark   Wee fuckin saps.

Tommy   'Junky'. 'Plaguer'.

Mark   Draftpak kids, thull harass anybody.

Tommy   You took the test?

Mark   Aye.

Tommy   Clear?

Mark   Aye.

Tommy   You used mair than me. And ye shared works.
Sick Boy's, Keezbo's, Raymie's, Spud's, Swanney's . . . ye
used Davie's fir fuck sake. Tell us ye nivir used Davie's works!

Mark   Ah nivir shared, Tommy.

Tommy   Bullshit! Cunt! You fuckin shared!

Mark Ah nivir shared . . .

Tommy Ah used tae sit n huv a bevvy wi Franco an a laugh at yis, call yis aw the daft cunts under the sun, fuckin junky. Then ah split fae Lizzy, mind? Went tae your bit. Ah asked ye fir a hit. Ah thoat, fuck it, ah'll try anythin once. Been trying it once ivir since.

Mark See . . . some cunts are so . . . predisposed tae smack.

Tommy Ah dinnae ken whit tae fuckin dae, Mark. Whit am ah gaunnae dae?

Mark Really sorry Tommy . . .

Tommy Goat any gear?

Mark Ah'm clean now, Tommy.

Tommy Sub us then, mate. Ah'm expectin a rent cheque.

Mark *puts money down.* **Tommy** *takes it and leaves, throwing the coat back at* **Mark**.

Mark Aw Tommy. Aw fucksakes. Ah didnae –
Ah wanted tae say 'Git oan wi yir life. It's aw ye can dae. Look eftir yirself'. But he willnae live fifteen, or ten or even five years before he's crushed by pneumonia or cancer. He's blown things wi his ma n he's here in one ay they hoatline jobs in West Granton. Fifteen thousand people oan the waitin list but naebody wanted this one. It's a prison. He willnae survive the winter. Sorry, mate. Ah'm really fuckin sorry.

Franco Ah'm fuckin Lee Marvin! Let's git some scran – and then hit a decent fuckin boozer.
Cummoan. Cummoan.

Franco *and* **Mark** *leave.*

Alison Whair ur ye gaun? Whair ur ye gaun?
Gaun tae the match, gaun tae the gig, gaun tae the pub wi mah mates, gaun doon tae London fir a few days, goat tae nash, gaun tae the airmy, tae Belfast, intae Bosnia, tae get doon tae some serious swedgin, ah wis fuckin game fir a

swedge, cummon ye crappin bastards!, ye big-moothed cunt,
yecuntchy, yecuntchy, cunt, cunt, cunt –

19

Alison   Ah'm walkin down the street wi Kelly, n these
guys, workies, up oan their scaffolding, whistle at us.
'Awright doll?'
Kelly's been doon tae see about her rent arrears n she's pretty
mad, like, tense n that, cos she turns oan the guy: 'Huv you
goat a girlfriend?' she shouts. 'Ah doubt it, because yir a fat
ugly prick!'
Aye! The guy looks at her wi real hate, I mean, now he's goat
a reason tae hate her, no jist cos she's a woman ken. The guys'
mates are gaun 'Whoooah, whoooah!' eggin him oan.
'Fuck off ya boot,' he snarls.
But she disnae, she stands her ground. 'O, ah wis a doll a
minute ago,' she cries, 'but now ah've telt ye tae fuck oaf
ah'm a boot. Well, you're still a fat ugly prick, son, and that's
no gaunnae change!'
(*Aussie*:) 'And so say all of us!' Australian lassie, wi a
backpack. A pair of thum. A few folk have stopped tae check
oot the hassle.
'Fuckin dykes!' another guy shouts.
Noo, that gets right oan ma tits, gettin called a dyke jist cos
ah object tae bein hassled by revolting ignorant radges.
'If all guys wir as repulsive as you, ah'e be fuckin proud tae be
a lesbian, son!' Did ah really say that? Crazy!
(*Aussie*:) 'You guys have obviously got a problem. Why don't
you just go and fuck each other?'
Quite a crowd has now gathered. Two auld wifies are
listening in. 'That's terrible' says one, 'lassies talkin like that
tae the laddies.'
'Och,' says the other wan, 'it's guid tae see lassies stickin up
fir thirsels. Wish it happened in ma day.' 'Aye,' she said tae
me, 'ah wish ah wis your age again hen, ah'd dae it aw
different, ah kin tell ye.'
The guys are looking embarrassed, really shit up by the
crowd. The foreman comes out 'Back inside yous!' And they

go, like sheep. And we aw let oot a cheer. It wis brilliant!
Magic!

Me and Kelly and the two Aussies and the two wifies all end
up in the Cafe Rio havin cups ay tea thegither. The Aussies
actually turned oot tae be New Zealanders, Veronica and
Jane. They *were* lesbians! Travelling round the world
thegither. Ah'd love tae gie that a go. Me and Kelly. Too
mad.

We take them back tae ma place fir a smoke ay hash. N we sit
there slaggin oaf men – stupid inadequate creatures wi flat
bodies and weird heids and dangling tubes. All thir guid fir is
the odd shag.

Sometimes ah wish ah wis gay. Dae it aw different.

What fuckin planet are we oan?

20

Sound: a ghostly train passes . . .

Franco   Lesh go fir a pish!

Alison   Three men meet in the ruins of old Leith Central
Station. Franco, Mark and the old drunkard who sleeps
there.

Franco   Some size ay a station this wis. Git a train tae
anywhere fae here at one time, so they sais.

Mark   Aye.

Franco   If it still hud fuckin trains, ah'd be oan one ah kin
tell ye, oot ay this fuckin dive.

Mark   Aye.

Franco   Real life, uh?

Drunk   What yis up tae lads? What yis up tae? Ye
trainspottin, ur ye?

Franco   Aye. That's right!

Drunk   Ah well, ah'll leave yis tae it.

Franco *grabs him, peers at his face and decks him.*

Drunk   Trainspottin . . .

Mark   Ah seen hum before.

Franco   Ma faither.

Mark   Whit?

Franco   He's ma faither. He's ma fuckin shitein faither!

Mark *and* **Franco** *piss* . . .

Mark   Trainspottin. Ah woke up in a strange bed in a strange room –

Sound: a train smashes through the scene, drowning him out.

Drugs

The original cast consulted the Gorbals Addiction Service, an agency which deals with local addicts on a daily basis, and from them we learned the process of 'cooking up' and injecting, and the physical and mental effects of the high and the withdrawal. All casts should do this kind of research; no printed explanation would suffice. It's worth mentioning, though, that we used the 2.5 ml syringe with the long (green) needle. For a first hit, Tommy would get 1 ml; there is a 1 ml syringe with a short (orange) needle. The trick is that no fluid is actually drawn into the syringe.

It should be mentioned that members of the audience have been known to faint in reaction to one or other of the injection scenes: it is wise to be prepared for this eventuality.

The play depicts the taking of speed [amphetamine sulphate, a white powder], heroin [a light brown powder], Ecstasy [white tablets], cannabis [peppermint tea mixed with cigarette tobacco gives a convincing odour] and large amounts of alcohol. The effect of Ecstasy is gradual, but the greater effect of light and sound at that point in the show means it's not necessary to play any delay.

David Stockley's *Drug Warning* (Optima Books, 1992), is an invaluable handbook on the signs and effects of drug use.

Headstate

**devised by the Boilerhouse Theatre Company
with Irvine Welsh**

Headstate was first performed at the Lemon Tree Theatre, Aberdeen, on 18 October 1994 by Boilerhouse Theatre Company with the following cast:

Martin Sykes	Tam Dean Burn
'John'	Jan Knightley
Tina Reed	Rachel Gartside
Mickey Crockertie	Christine Devaney

Director Paul Pinson
Designer Karen Tennent
Lighting George Tarbuck
Music Graham Cunnington

Headstate was devised by

Tam Dean Burn
Graham Cunnington
Christine Devaney
Rachel Gartside
Jan Knightley
Paul Pinson
Karen Tennent
George Tarbuck
Irvine Welsh

Characters

Martin Sykes
'John'
Tina Reed
Mickey Crockertie

Scene One

*In the club. The performers are merged with the audience who are led
into the space. It is a club with loud house music, lights and dry ice. The
performers are at first very friendly and dance, and create a vibe.*
Mickey *does not interact with the rest. She has a ghostly, angelic
image as she goes around filming and questioning people.*

Martin (*to audience, dancing*)   I just come here a lot. I don't
come to get off with anybody, I just come to dance. No really
intae shagging these days, eh.
I've got a shop, a butcher's like. Cannae be bothered though,
eh. Havnae opened the fuckin place for weeks. The stock'll
be ruined. It'll be fuckin boggin in there man!
Three doves last night . . . and one of they speedballs.
Wasted likes. Pure cunted.
How did you get here?

John (*to audience, dancing*)   I was treated like a dog. I'm an
articulate guy. I can express myself. People get the wrong
idea about me. That's the problem. There's nothing wrong
with my mouth. I'm not wearing girls' underpants. I don't
need all that. Do you come here often? How did you get here?
Do you think anybody could love someone like me. I mean,
like as I am now?
How did you get here?

Tina (*to audience, dancing*)   Hiya!
Got any kids?
I've got two. They're really beautiful, really really beautiful
kids. I mean, I know everybody thinks that about their kids,
but I mean, if you saw my kids, they're really great. I really
love them. You've got to have somebody to love, haven't
you?
How did you get here?

John *sees* **Mickey** *filming. At first he freaks out. Then he runs
through the crowd to find the others to inform them of her 'resurrection'.
He is slowly becoming inarticulate and changing into a dog. He finds*

Martin, *but finds it hard to explain that he has 'seen'* **Mickey**.
Martin, **John** *and* **Tina** *leave the club*.

Mickey   How much can you afford?

Scene Two

John, **Tina** *and* **Martin** *return to a flat where* **Mickey**'*s dead body is on a table*.

Martin   See John, there she is. It couldnae have been her in the club, no unless she had taken one of these speedballs and whizzed round before we got our coats.

Tina   She's still here, you sick bastards.

John   She's dead. Dead.

Martin   Gie her some of these fuckin doves n speedballs, they'll get her going!

Tina   Shut it! Shut up!

Martin   I'm only joking Tina . . . fuck sake, I'm off ma fuckin tits here, like.

John   It's not fair . . . it's not fair.

Martin   Aye, well life's no fuckin well fair, is it?

Tina   You've still got her here. You sad bastards.

Martin   We're getting it sorted.

Tina   You've still fucking well got her here! You fucking sick bastards!

John (*mumbled, tugging at* **Martin**)   She can't be wasted . . .

Martin   Look, it's you that's fuckin wasted, ya daft cunt. I'm going to get rid of it. I'll dismember her.

Tina   What are you fucking well on about? What are you going to do? Are you going to chop this bit off, or that bit off?

Martin   I'm a butcher. I know about meat.

John   Meat . . . she's just like a fucking piece of meat . . .

Martin (*gets some meat from fridge to distract* **John**) Here . . .

Tina What did he say?

Martin The guy's a fuckin nutter. Ignore him. A total fuckin reality bypass, that's what that cunt suffers from. He thinks he's a dog, he dresses up like a fucking tart . . .

Tina We killed her! We fucking well killed her!

Martin That nutter, that stupid, demented, self-centred egotistical slag, she caused all the problems in the first place . . . (*Goes over to body* . . .)
You fucking slut. You got everything you wanted, everything you asked for . . . we could have been in the clear now doll. No, you had to spoil everything, didn't you, you horrible disgusting fucker.

Tina How did we get into this?

Martin How did I get here, with all these fuckin bams? How did I get here?

Tina Fuck you, how did I get here? What am I doing here? I don't know anything . . . I don't know who the fuck I am . . . I don't know who the fuck I am!

Scene Three

The 'clothes tunnel'. This focuses on **Tina**'s *attempt to fill various roles.*

Mickey Look at her, making herself beautiful to meet the perfect man, to plant the perfect seed, to make the perfect child . . .

. . . But she was never happy. Always something wrong. Wrong make-up, wrong style, wrong colour; so wrong man, wrong seed, wrong baby . . .

. . . wrong woman.

Hi Tina, how are you today?

Tina Hi Mickey. I'm fine.

Mickey   Have you thought about what you want today?

Tina   What I want today . . . huh . . . I want everybody to look out for each other.

Mickey   We all want that Tina.

Tina   Yeah, but it's not possible is it?

Mickey   Maybe it is possible.

Tina   No, it would take everyone to do it at the same time.

Mickey   Yes, but that has to start somewhere. Maybe it has to start with you, Tina. Maybe it has to start with you.

Tina   Maybe you're right. Maybe she is right.

Scene Four

The past: 'Tina's Story'. This is told fairy story style. Tina is in the centre of the floor shooting up on heroin. The other characters are invisible but provide dialogue.

Mother   Our little darling.

Father   We love her so much.

Dog   I'm a dog and even I love her.

Tina   And I love you too Mummy, Daddy and woof-woof and everybody in the whole wide world!

Father   Our little Princess.

At school.

Teacher   Well done Tina! Another gold star!

Pupil One   I wish I was as clever as her.

Pupil Two   I hate the cunt.

Teacher   Tina shall certainly go to University and secure excellent qualifications and get a fine job, although she's so lovely and good and fine, that I fully expect that some rich and handsome Prince will fall in love with her before then.

Enter her Prince/Lover.

Prince/Lover   Darling!

Tina   Wow! A Prince! He's a bit of alright n all. What about a shag?

Prince/Lover   Oh Tina . . . no need to rush things. Let me read you this poem: 'I wandered lonely, as a cloud . . .'

Tina   Fuck your poem, I've an itchy pussy here . . . my lover is so boring with his poetry and his good intentions. I want danger, I want excitement, I want a good shag and to get off my tits on chemicals of all sorts.

Enter the **Dragon**.

Dragon   Come with me and ignore that puff of a Prince, doll. Chase me around a wee bit. Fuck all those daft cunts. They don't understand you Tina. We'll have a bit of fun, eh babes?

Tina (*to* **Prince**)   If you love me truly then you will slay the Dragon.

The **Prince** *tries vainly but cannot repel the* **Dragon**.

Prince/Lover   I cannot complete this task my love, the Dragon is too strong . . .

Tina   Oh go away you useless git. Oh . . . what can I do about this Dragon?

Witch laugh. Enter **Witch**.

Tina   Mummy . . .

Witch   I'm not your mummy . . .

Tina   You're a witch!

Witch   You must have a child Tina. There are emotional and financial benefits. You must have a child to indulge your ego and produce a perfect being who will not be fucked up by you like you were by your repressed mummy and daddy.

Tina   So I get to shag tons of blokes?

Witch   Yes. But use a condom Tina. Except when you make the babies, of course.

Tina   Yeeaasss!

Dragon   Tina . . . you have two children . . .

Tina   But I only really wanted one. Two's too much like hard work . . . all my friends are partying. I want to party!

Tina *gives her babies to people in the audience.*

Tina   Please look after my babies. Take care of them for me. I love them so much. Don't let anybody else take them. Look after them, please. You will look after them, won't you?

Enter **Officials**. *They approach* **Tina**.

Official One   Where are your children Tina? David Phillip Reed, and Jessica Jane Reed. Where are the babies Tina?

Tina   Why?

Official Two   Where are they Tina?

Tina   They're being looked after!

Official One   Where?

Tina   It's nothing to do with you. They're being cared for.

Official Two   Where are they being cared for?

Tina   They're being cared for in the community!

Official One   You can't look after them, can you Tina?

Tina   Yes I can!

Official One   We have to take them Tina, we have to keep them safe. Look, we've been through this before. We know you don't have sufficient maturity or the financial security to look after them.

The **Officials** *repeat this phrase which is hammered home by the other 'official' voice through the speakers. The* **Officials** *then go to the members of the audience and take the babies, repeating the phrase in response to any objections.*

Scene Five

The flat. The present.

Martin   It's for the best Tina, the babies.

Tina   Fuck off.

John (*sniffing body*)   I love her.

Martin (*kicking* **John**)   Get the fuck away fae there!

Tina   John . . . he's a fucking freak.

John   I want her . . .

Martin (*snapping at* **John**)   Leave that fuckin body John!
I'm fucking tellin ye!

Tina   I want my babies . . . I want my mum . . . my dad
. . . what's happening to me? What's gone wrong with
everything? I want my babies!

Martin   Look, we need tae get some bread the gither. I'll
help ye get it sorted out. I'll help ye get them back . . . fuck
. . . I'll need tae get that shop open . . .

John (*cowering away*)   She's mine . . .

Tina   She's fucking nobody's. She's just another drug.
Makes you feel good for a while, then it fucks you right up.

John *mounts the body again.*

Martin   I fucking well telt ye, leave her ya daft cunt!
(*Steams into* **John** *and gives him a kicking. Interrupted by the phone
ringing.*)

Tina (*tending* **John**)   You're a fucking pig, Martin. What's
going on with you? You never used to be like that . . . he
didn't, John, he never used to be like that . . .

John   I just want her back . . .

Martin (*into phone*)   Hi Al.
Awright.
Aye.
Aye.

Ah'm needing a couple of weeks grace Al. One or two wee
complications.
Yeah (*Looks at* **Mickey**.) . . . she's fine. Got to look after our
investment, eh Al?
Naw, naw . . . dinnae get ays wrong Al. It's just that we had
to spend a bit of time getting the flat done up, Mickey
couldn't entertain anybody in a shithouse.
Oh aye, I'll be getting the other chicks on line a.s.a.p., but it's
a special skill. Mind, it's no sex we're selling, it's love. That's
why I'm spending so much time in the clubs Al, trying to get
it on with some of these wee party chicks. They've got to be
special though Al, they've got to have that maturity . . . they
need to be understanding and intelligent. This is
interpersonal skills intensive work we're talking about here,
yeah? That's the scam. This isnae just steaming in tae clubs
Al, getting heat fae polis n that. This is enterprise in its purest
form.
Message received and understood Al. Have I ever let ye
down before?
Right Al, see ye mate. Keep in touch. And don't worry. It's
all in hand.
(*Puts phone down.*)
Fuck! What are we gaunny dae!

Tina We're going to be completely fucked.

John I want to go home.

Martin You've nae fuckin hame tae go tae ya daft cunt.
(*Kicks* **John** *again.*) And that fuckin hoor; fucked the whole
thing right up!

Martin *switches on horror video on TV.*
The phone rings again. He answers it, leaving **Tina** *watching the
video.*

John I've no home to go to . . .

Scene Six

John's story. *The past. He is rescued from violence by his future wife. During seduction he becomes violent to her. She leaves, he sniffs her dress. Then he commits a violent act which is witnessed by* **Martin**. **Martin** *is a former casual involved in the clubscene. He offers* **John** *a job if he is prepared to be his dog.*

Martin (*narrates* **John**'s *story on phone*)   Aw, it's you again Al. What? John? Aw aye, dinnae worry aboot John. He's either at your feet or at your throat, so I keep the cunt at my feet.
Naw, he could hardly speak English when he came here. Fae some Commie country, Russia or somewhere like that. Ah mean, I don't think the guy's the maist articulate cunt in the world at the best of times. Some sort ay speech impediment, but the poor cunt didnae ken the lingo. He got intae some bother back fae where he came fae. Did something tae somebody, a lassie I think.
Naw.
He's sound though.
Naw, some fuckin bitch, some well-meaning do-gooder *Guardian*-reader type, some fuckin middle-class cunt who read aboot him and thought it would be great to sponsor him, tae get him ower here. Sort of rescue the poor wretch from the clutches of oppression in one of the far off hell-holes of Eastern Europe, if ye get my drift. So that's the daft cunt set up, a tidy bird n aw. She's chuffed. A wee bit ay rough for her.
But I told you about John, he's a bit of a psycho cunt, he starts getting aw heavy wi her and she gets a bit bored with him, so she takes him for a car ride into the country, then fuckin dumps him, just like you'd dae tae a dug. Tells him to fuck off. So the poor cunt's stranded here on his puff, just like he was back hame.
(*As* '**Wife**' *runs off.*)
Aw aye.
So the poor bastard's wandering lost, not a clue where he's going, cold and hungry, until he comes across a town. All the

daft fucker wanted was a Big Mac and a Coke. That was what the stupid cunt thought the west was all about. It was like his symbol of freedom. He got one n all. The daft cunt was chuffed to bits sitting in the garish neon lit shit-house surrounded by schemies in shell-suits and screaming brats, with their miserable chain-smoking tranquilised mothers. Aye, daft John thought this was freedom. The toxic hamburger and corrosive liquid burning in his guts. He was eating shit, but he was happy in a strange way. Then he realised that to keep doing this was a problem. One: you needed money and you dinnae get any without a job. Two: there were no jobs for him. He started taking the McDonalds that people threw away in the bins. He lived off them. They were the only half-eaten food that people seemed to throw away. That was because they were shite. John never wanted to eat McDonald's again.

I know, I know. Poor bastard.

It was grim, but in the town, he ran into me. I saw him sorting out these cunts that were trying tae give him grief. He was tidy. Just a wee bit crazy. Me and Andy were trying tae get the club up and running and we'd been having a bit of bother. I gave him a job, as a bouncer. He was good with the punters. Took it easy, but was tasty when he needed to be. He was like my fuckin dog. I'd just set him on any cunt that messed.

Thing was, and this is weird, but he kept hearing voices. He kept hearing his wife, this trendy cow, talking tae him. It was like he didnae want tae believe that she had left him. He kept setting the table for two. Thing was, he had got some of her clothes.

Aye.

Aye, he kept hearing her voice. Telling him to touch the clothes, to wear them even, like it brought them closer. He put them on. I caught him once. That's another thing I've got on him.

Dinnae worry.

John's sound. The money's nae problem Al. We'll get it sorted out our end. This is gaunny be big.

Scene Seven

The flat. The present.

Tina   So you exploited John.

Martin   Did I fuck exploit him. John's a mate. John and I
are close buddies. Sorry I fuckin well flipped there John . . .
I'm fuckin edgy. It's just all this shite . . . eh! A fuckin
corpse on ma table! Nae wonder I'm fuckin edgy eh! I'm
takin another half a dove. We need love vibes here. Posse
vibes, that's the answer. That's the only thing that'll sort
this mess oot. John . . . fucking brilliant. I fuckin well love
John man.

Tina   So you're fucking John these days then, Martin?

Martin   Actually darling, one isn't fucking well fucking
anyone these days.

Scene Eight

Martin*'s story. The past. The opening sequence shows* **Martin** *in*
Karaoke. He comes on as a stand-up comic.

Martin   Awright my friends, Sykesie's the name. Ten
years of yobbery and eight years of clubbing. Acid House? I
fuckin invented it man. Some say it started in 1988, others
say 1987 others say 1986. It's all bollocks of course. House
started the day Martin Sykes was pulled out of his Ma's
womb. It's aw been one big fuckin perty since then and the
rest of the world can tune in, or jump out as and when it
fuckin well likes.
So I'm gaunny tell a few gags, sing a couple of old
numbers you all know so well. I've got my lovely assistant
John here, come on John, give us a twirl! That's enough
ya daft cunt!
Now I'm HIV, right? Too much banging up wi shared
needles back in the eighties. So a lot of my mates have
now got AIDS. The first guy I knew who had it, I'm up

seeing the poor bastard in the hospice. This is when they knew fuck all about AIDS, right? So I said to him: how are the cunt's treating you my man?

He goes, well Martin, cannae complain. Everyone's fine. Understanding, sympathetic. Great staff. There is one thing though.

What's that? I goes.

The boy says, well, they keep giving me toast. Breakfast, dinner and tea, it's always toast.

How's that? I asked him.

Well Martin, he says, it's the only thing they can slide under the fuckin door!

Anyway, this an old Stooges number, so feel free to sing along . . .

Martin *starts to sing along to 'Dirt', talking to the audience during the guitar passages.*

I feel it alright. I've maybe always had it. There was always something inside me. A wee imaginary friend growing inside me. It turned into my Ma one time, that was just after she died.

All I wanted was a laugh. I was into action, with the cashies n that. I could mobilise the boys. Organisation, that's what appealed. Organising violence. Being somebody. Then that got a drag, too much polis hassle. They put me away. I got into house, into Ecky. Brilliant. I met a lot of lassies. Tina tae name but one. It was sound. Thing is, I shot smack a few times with some of them from her crowd . . . just for something tae dae, eh.

Just a couple of times. I wisnae a junkie. Ecky was my drug. But there's me HIV positive, and that cow's okay. Fuckin weird life.

My imaginary friend. Growing inside me.

I talked to you a lot in prison. There was nobody else.

Martin 2 (Aids Voice)   You're a bit of a fuck up, aren't you?

Martin Yeah, that's because of you. Dragging around an arsehole like you limits one's possibilities.

> **Martin 2** Don't you think that's a little too convenient, Martin? I got you sent to jail, I lost you the shops, I got your girlfriend to take your child to Ibiza, I got you into the casuals, I got you into skag, I got you HIV. All that's left is just poor, nice unfucked up old Martin.

Martin That's right! That's fucking right! I've never fucked anybody over in my life but if you fuckin well stand still they take the piss out of you, you've got to be fuckin strong . . . why don't you just come out, get it over with . . .

> **Martin 2** It's not as easy as that Martin. I need you as much as you need me.

Martin Why do I need you?

> **Martin 2** I can be your excuse, your excuse for almost anything . . .

Martin And then my auld man died . . . I had to take over the fuckin butchers shop. I didn't want that . . . I didn't want any of that shite . . . going into work strung out after raving all weekend, trying to put a cheery face on to all the daft auld cunts who wanted me to be a replica of my auld man . . . one thing it taught me was that we are all game. That's live meat, waiting to be transformed into dead meat. Great, eh.

> **Martin 2** That old bastard that comes in. Her nasty, coothie, wizened face Martin. Judging you, adding to your strung-out pain with her vicious, disapproving scowls.

Martin   That auld cunt Mrs Thomson . . .

> **Martin 2**   Give her your
> blood Martin. Give it to her in
> your sausages. Infect the
> meat.

Martin   Naw . . . ye cannae fuckin dae that . . .

> **Martin 2**   Infect the meat.

Martin   But . . .

> **Martin 2**   Infect the meat.

Martin   Aye . . . why not . . . here you go Mrs Thomson,
here's the sausages. Ay, it's a bit colder this morning. There's
a wee chill in the air.
There's a chill.

John *covers him with clothes.*

Scene Nine

Tina *is talking to* **Mickey**'s *corpse.*

Tina   You told me that it was all possible, and I knew that
it wasn't possible. You stupid daft cow. You know, I don't
know if you are really stupid or a fucking liar. But you messed
my head right up with your mind games. Now you're dead.
Who was right? You're stiffed. I rest my fucking case.

Tina *moves over to* **Martin** *as* **John** *is pining and howling over*
Mickey's *corpse.*

Look at you. She's dead. Your business partner. All you can
think about is how to make money out of her. Why don't you
just drain off her blood and pump her full of formaldehyde?
Stick her under a sunlamp and sell her for a tenner a fuck.

Martin   You'd like that, eh? You'd like to see her used in
that way. That would give you your kicks, wouldn't it you
fucking sick, jealous cow.

Mickey *resurrects and starts filming. Only* **John** *sees her.* **Tina** *and* **Martin** *are blethering away and pay* **John** *no heed. He follows her.* **Mickey** *starts talking to the audience.*

Mickey   I sold love, not sex. I thought about selling sex, but it's not what people want. They want love, but they don't value it unless they can pay for it. Anything free has no value, because the market puts a value on everything. To consume is to be free.
Who do you love?

Mickey *then approaches* **Martin**. *All the time she is being followed by a sniffing* **John**.

Mickey   Who do you love, Martin?
He's so fucked up he wouldn't know love if it bit him on the cock.
Martin. Can you hear me? Can you feel me?
This wanker wouldn't know what love was if it slapped him in the face. (*Slaps him.*)

Martin (*to* **Tina**)   What about crashing out for a bit? You and me like.

Tina   Nah, I'm not into that any more . . .

Martin   There was time you werenae so fuckin particular.

Tina   What the fuck are you saying? What's wrong with you? Look at us! Look at this!

Martin   So you're Snow White again, eh?

Tina   I don't fucking well know what I am.

They continue their discussion while **Mickey** *goes across to* **John**.

Mickey   He doesn't know about love. He doesn't understand.
But if I tell him what to do, he'll do it.
Show me some love.
Show me some love.
He's obedient, like a dog. Servile. If I tell him what to do he'll do it. But I don't believe him.
But what he wants to do is . . . fuck. Is that not right, John?

John   No, I'm not like that. I love you.

Mickey   Ha! What happened to you, John. Someone has loved you though, haven't they?

John   Pretended to.

Mickey   Did.

John   No.

Mickey   He won't believe it. This one's confused. How would you love then, John?

John   What . . .

Mickey   Show me, John, show me how you would love . . . (*They start having sex.*) He thinks if he has a good fuck he's finding love, he thinks that his heart will be at ease.

John   I love you . . .

Mickey   He thinks a shag will do it for him . . . (*Breaks away.*) YOU CAN'T SHAG ME LIKE I'M A PIECE OF MEAT! IT'S NOT LOVE!

John   C'mon . . .

Mickey   It's okay baby . . .

They embrace and shag a bit more then **Mickey** *leaves the sleeping* **John** *and goes over and grabs* **Martin** *whom she pushes towards* **Tina**.

Tina   Do I look good for you?

Martin   Yeah, phoah, you'll fucking well do me!

Tina   But do I look good for you?

Martin   Yeah, fucking well told you so, now get em off!

Tina   Fuck you!

Martin   No, fuck you!

Tina   Get out my fucking sight, get away from me, go on!

Martin   What's got into you, you fucking daft whore, you some fucking carpet-muncher or something? Fuck off!

Tina You fucking sad prick . . . just fuck off you fucking clueless tosser!

Martin Fucking dirty cock teasing slag; you're all the fucking same!

Tina Alright then, fuck me. Let's go to bed. Or maybe across the table here. Have you got the bottle? I bet you fucking well haven't! There's something going on with you, isn't there? C'mon then, fuck me!

Martin (*backing away*) I can't . . . I just can't . . .

Tina Ha!

Mickey (*to audience*) They still care enough to feel strongly about things. This is where I get my fucking kicks. It proves that something's still going on inside there. It's still there; some sort of passion. It's warped, it's twisted and it's perverted, but it's still there. As long as it is there are possibilities that it can become something else. Something better.

Scene Ten

John *is in* **Mickey**'s *room. She is narrating.*

Mickey Of course, when John came to me he was even more messed up than he was now. He was one of my clients. One of my most interesting clients.
Hello Joanne. How are you?

John I'm fine.

Mickey So what do you want today, Joanne?

John Love.

Mickey In what way?

John I want . . . I want a sister. I had two brothers, both older than me. I want a sister to love.

Mickey You've had brothers, Joanne, but no sister. That means you don't know what it's like to have a sister. Would you want to fuck your sister? Would you want to make love to her, Joanne?

John   No . . . yes . . . I might . . .

Mickey   Cause if you want a sister, it's not a real sister you want. Is it a mother you want, Joanne?

John (*frightened, regressing into dog*)   Mhhmmhmmm . . . mhmmmhmm . . .

Mickey   It's alright Joanne, don't worry. I love you Joanne.

John   Mhmmmm. Mhmmmm. Mhmmmm.

Mickey   You have a voice Joanne, whose voice is it?

> **Voice in John's Head**   She's charging you forty quid an hour and she still won't come across for you, John. You're soft.

John   GRRRRR!!

Mickey   Stop it Joanne. Listen to me. I love you Joanne.

John   Nooooo! I'm not a real woman! My name's John!

Mickey   No, you're not a real woman. You're a very handsome man, John. You're just frightened baby, aren't you? Just frightened because nobody's ever loved you properly.
I love you John.
I love you.
Mickey loves you John.

John   No!

Mickey   I do.
Mickey four John.
I'll always be there for you baby, always there to pick you up when you feel down. There's a bond between us, John. A bond of love. Can you feel it, John? Can you feel it?

Voice in John's Head If she loved you she'd let you fuck her. She's just like the nasty slag who brought you here John. You're just a sodding toy to her. Forty quid John. You're on one pound seventy an hour in security work. A week's wages John, a weeks wages and you don't even get to fuck her. You're a refugee John. You've seen things they can't imagine, things you don't want to remember. The soldiers John. Remember them? What did they do to you, John?

John GRRRRLLLL!

Mickey I'm not going to shout at you, John. They all shout at you darling. They all shout at you because they don't love you like I do. Tear my throat out if you want. Is that what you want? Do what you want John. I love you. Do what you want.

Voice in John's Head Do it! Tear her throat out and fuck her!

Mickey Do it John. Show them all what a brutalised piece of shit you are. Conform to their view of you. It's just John, stupid, silly John, incapable of any finer feelings, incapable of anything other than shitting, pissing, shagging, eating, come on John, tear my throat out. Destroy love. Go on John, destroy it.

Voice in John's Head Do it! What are you fucking waiting on!

Mickey Do it.

Voice in John's Head   Do
it!

Mickey   Do it!

Voice in John's Head   Do
it!

John   No! I love her! I love you! (*Collapses in* **Mickey**'s
arms.)

Mickey   It's alright . . . it's alright. We've all been there
before, all of us. We've all known what the hurt's like.

Scene Eleven

This physical scene takes place in imaginative space. **Mickey** *is
dispossessed by the other members of the cast. Her personal items are
taken away, and she is eventually stripped of her clothing by them.
This hints at but does not make explicit a possible child-abuse
background.*

Scene Twelve

The three characters blind-search for **Mickey***, they find her and open
their eyes. This scene is neither past nor present but functions in an
imaginative space which is possibly a collective drug-induced
psychosis.*

Scene Thirteen

The flat. Three way interactive love scene. Builds up into crescendo.
John *and* **Tina** *fade down as* **Martin** *opens up. The characters
repeat the following statements.*

John   I can control myself now. I just want her to be happy.
I'm not like that now. I'm different. I'm better. I understand
now.

Tina I just want people to look out for each other, but it's not possible because everybody has to do it at the same time.

Mickey It is possible.
Let me in.
Let me in Martin, come on. You said we could help each other, that you could be of use to me and I could be of use to you. Let me in.

Martin We can really clean up doll. I could make you so fuckin big, but the thing is, can you handle it?

Micky Yeah, but you have to trust me, you have to let me in . . .

Martin It's got to be on a business level doll. Strictly fuckin business.

Mickey Yes Martin, but you have to believe in the product, you have to let me in. If you're going to sell a product successfully, you have to believe in it. Do you believe in love, Martin?

Martin If love can be sold, I believe in love. If love enhances profit. I believe in it.

Mickey Then let me in Martin . . . to believe it you have to feel it. Can you feel it?

Martin You wouldnae be able to get in. Naebody can.

Mickey I can. With your help I can. You can let me in. You have to let me in Martin, you have to sample the wares . . .

Martin Yes . . . oh yes . . . Mickey . . .

> **Martin 2** You can't let them in . . . they just fuck you up . . . they just fuck you up . . . I'm a butcher . . . we're all meat . . . meat is all there is . . . we can be bought and sold. We have to use everything up. Every piece of

the carcass has its use.
Nothing must be wasted. It's
waste that holds us back . . .

John and *Tina* *fade out.*

Martin   No, its not like that
You showed me love
I came to you and you showed me love
I saw your card
I came to make money and you gave me love . . .
love
love
love

Martin 2   But she still fuckin
charged you for it, didn't she?
What's her percentage of the
business Martin? Who's in
control here? Where does the
power lie?

Martin   No!

Martin 2   You're dirt. It's
all inside. Can you feel it,
Martin? You had bad shits
last night. You sweated
Martin. Can you feel me
coming? Can you feel me
coming out more, everytime
you open up?

Martin *springs over to* **John** *and* **Tina**.

Martin   The cunt's fucking with our heads.

John   She loves us?

Martin   She's screwing us in our fuckin wallets! That was
what it's all about!

John   I love her . . .

Martin   Fuck her. It's just a job to her.

Tina   She used you.

John   No . . . where did she go . . .

Martin   Forget her. She uses people. She fucks up their heads, damages them.

Tina   That's what she does, it's all a fucking game to her.

Martin   She doesn't love you!

John   No! I love her! Where is she?

Tina   She's away with someone else.

Martin   Someone with a whole lot more money than you, pal. It's a scam, you fuckin donut! A scam: love for fucking sale. You went along to her place and believed all that shite. Just because you missed your wife and she reminded you of her.

John   No . . . she wouldn't . . .

Tina   She fucked us over too. Can't you get that into your fucking thick head? She uses people. It's how she gets her kicks. She's just another power junky.

John   I don't believe you . . .

Martin   It's just another fucking scam mate, that's all it is.

Tina   Oh, I'm sure she made you feel special. That's her job.

Martin   Oh she's crafty alright. Don't you see, that's what makes her dangerous. She has to be stopped.

Tina   You can do it. You have to do it for yourself.

Martin   Yeah, it's about taking things into your own hands. Nobody can help you but you. C'mon John, you can do it. The old days when I used to run with the boys, now that was excitement. That was feeling alive. Sort the fucking bitch out, John. Sort her out for all those bitches that fucked up your head and mad_ , ou into a fucking dog.

Scene Fourteen

The flat. The past.

Martin You fuckin slag . . . you rip us off and you fuck
with our heads . . .

Mickey You don't understand . . . you're fucking
primitives the lot of you. You want to buy your fucking
trinkets, your silly little gadgets to make you happy. You
vote for any cynical cunt who you think is going to take the
less from you in tax possible so you can buy more shite you
don't want to impress wankers you hate, while they shit all
over you!

Tina Yeah, people like you who shit all over us you fucking
whore!

Martin *and* **Tina** *start attacking* **Mickey**.

Martin John! Get her boy! Get her! She fucked you over
John boy! Get her John, go on boy!

John *joins attack.*

Martin Fuck us over, would you?

John See how you like it cunt!

Tina Whore!

Martin Fuckin cunt!

John Dirty lying fucking cow!

Martin Fuck us over, would you?

John See how you like it cunt!

Tina Whore!

Martin Fuck us over, would you? Fuckin bitch, that'll
teach ye!

John You cunt!

Mickey *is still. She is dead.*

Scene Fifteen

They are standing over **Mickey***'s dead body.*

Martin   C'mon. You did this n aw.

Tina   You started it.

John   Why did you go . . . sorry . . . why did you go . . .
sorry . . . please . . . don't do this . . . come back . . . please
. . . come back . . .

Martin *starts to wrap body in clingfilm.*

Martin   Keep it fresh.

Tina   What are you doing?

Martin   Keep her fresh. Might be able to do something
with her . . .

Tina   Like what?

Martin   Give us a hand. You did this as well.

Tina   What do you mean, do something?

Martin   Like revive her or something . . . I don't know
about these things. It's just best to try to keep her fresh.
C'mon, give us a hand.

Tina   I don't want to.

Martin   There's something inside her for sure. Let's keep
her fresh so that it willnae spoil. We'll be able to get it out of
her.

Tina   She's dead.

John   Dead . . .

Martin   We can get the thing out of her later.

John   What do you mean. How?

Martin   I dunno, cut it out or something. Not now. We can
keep her fresh. There must be something we can use.

John   Yes . . . everything has to be used. There has to be no
waste.

Tina What the fuck's going on here!

Martin That's it John, it's waste that's the killer!
Everything is a potential resource, everything has value.
She's probably more useful to me as she is. Know what I
mean?

John No . . .

Martin Ever shag her?

John No.

Martin Nor me. I could go giving her one now though.

Tina You sick bastard!

Martin Look, she's fuckin stiffed. I'm HIV. Where am I
going to get a jump without fucking anyone else over? I could
do it now.

Tina What are you talking about? What are you talking
about? HIV? When? When were you HIV!

Martin Way after you and I were together. Don't you
fuckin worry. I've not been with anyone since I found out
. . . her though . . . she's still warm. I want a fuckin shag
before I go . . . and you John, you must be desperate for a
hump. That slag who teased you, now here's your chance to
settle that account in full . . .

John Eh . . .

Martin While she's still warm.

John I don't know . . . I would have to go first. . . .

Martin Go on!

Tina Fuck off! Don't piss about you bastards. I'm still up
here . . . those fucking doves. C'mon, let's have a dance.
Keep dancing that's the secret. Hardcore. Dance your way
through all this fucking horrible shit.

They dance, **John** *holding* **Mickey***'s corpse up. We move into the
present.*

Scene Sixteen

The flat, the present. **John** *has strapped* **Mickey** *up to some sort of trolley so that she is vertical and he can dance with her at his ease.*

John (*to audience*)   She was a good person. Her heart was pure. She tried to do things that would help people. She helped me.

Simultaneously, **Martin** *and* **Tina** *are talking* . . .

Martin   You can understand it with that poor cunt, falling for her fuckin nonsense. I should have known better.

Tina   So should I.

Martin   Hmmmpf.

Tina   What's that supposed to mean?

Martin   Disnae mean anything.

Tina   No Martin, tell me. Tell what you're fucking well driving at!

Martin   Awright, ah will fuckin tell ye! It means that you're a typical fucked-up middle-class cow who had it all on a plate and then decided that mummy and daddy didn't understand ye. I've no fuckin sympathy with you, it's just another wee fad for you to indulge yourself on. I can see you now, oh, I think I'll have some love for sale . . . you don't know what real life is!

Tina   I've had my fucking children taken away! Don't fucking well tell me what I know and what I don't fucking well know!

Martin   Your children. That was just another fucking fad Tina; I want a little baby. Everyone make a fuss of Tina, the centre of attention. Then when the fucked-up bitch had to look after them, what happened? The dopey cow just wanted to party. Poor fucking Tina. Two lives fucking ruined because poor Tina wants to party!

Tina   You bastard . . . you don't know me. You don't fuckin know me at all.

Martin I do Tina. I know you exactly.

Tina You think you've got it all sussed. Well tell us, mister perfectly healthy businessman, mister sophisticated entrepreneur: what's life all about?

Martin Life's about . . . meat.

Tina Fuck off! Meat! The only thing that's meat is your brains Martin. You've been working in that fucking shop too long!

Martin We live as live game, we die as meat. All her shit about love. Love, community, all that shit, it's been taken over by the profit system. In its industrial infancy capitalism could co-exist uneasily with love and community. These things have been around much longer than the profit system. But that system, once it found its fuckin strength, its maturity, in consumerism, it just eats them up. It eats up everything. It shapes it all to its own ends. Love, community, they're all just fuckin scams now. They don't exist on their own. They exist as part of something, the bottom line of which is money, is profit.

Tina Listen baby, I love it when you talk politics. Politics and meat, that's what I need, sexual politics and loads of fucking throbbing red meat. C'mon, let's fuck, like we used to.

Martin Look, I don't fuck anymore. I'm not into it . . . I can't.

Tina But you did it. You used the condoms.

Martin (*produces gun*) Condoms leak! Condoms split! Condoms burst! There's no safe sex for me, no fuckin safe haven any more. We're one fuckin thrust from obliteration! Twice I banged up. Twice, that's all. Twice I shared. With the wrong cunts! Mitch, Tony . . . cunts you introduced me to! Mind that? I wasn't a desperate junky, itching for a fix, and fuck the consequences. You used more fuckin skag in one session than I did in a lifetime! Blow the cunts away! Blow them all away! They're fuckin dead meat! Let some other cunt sort it all out!

Tina   She blew you away, didn't she?

Martin   What about you? What did she say to you when you saw her?

Tina   I needed her.

Martin   So?

Tina   So she made me feel small when she wanted to make me feel good. She thought she was love; special, a Godess. When you meet a Godess, how do you feel in response? You feel totally fucking inadequate. That was the thing, she was setting herself up as superior, as better than us. That's the role of gods, the self-righteous role.

Martin   She was though.

Tina   Fuck off, how? How was she better than us?

Martin   Because we paid for her services. The market. She sold something to make us better. It was a great thing. We could have been minted her and I.

Tina   I remember her kindness . . .

Scene Seventeen

The present. They have all been taking more Ecstasy.

Tina   I'm rushing like fuck . . . I need a shit . . . no I don't . . . ha ha ha . . . I might take another half.

Martin   You know, the more I think of it, the more I think you were right. I can get her blood drained off and get her filled up with formaldehyde. That would be brilliant. Then we could get the adverts in the specialist magazines. Everything can be sold. There are people who can only come with a passive wank object. They pay for the sex, not the interaction. I read somewhere that most necrophiliacs have cocks measuring less than two inches. Cunts with wedding tackle like that don't want anybody who can move around or whoops . . .

Tina   Whoops-a-daisy . . . sorry love, just slipped out again . . .

Martin   That's it . . . the passive fuck. And aw the cunts wi AIDS who want a poke but dinnae want tae risk infecting anybody! There is a necromarket! Has to be!

There is the sound of a letter coming through the door.

Tina   What the fuck's that?

Martin (*picks up mail and opens it*)   Chill oot, it's only the fuckin post.
Ha ha ha . . . it's fae the environmental health cunt's up at the council. 'Dear Mister Sykes, Re: 22 Main Street Anytown. We are responding to complaints from fellow traders and from passers-by regarding the unpleasant smell which appears to be coming from your shop at the above address. It seems that this shop has not been open for some time for trading purposes. If some stock has been left unattended you appreciate that this is a potential public health hazard. As a statutory authority we are invested with the powers of enforced entry to the above premises. In order to avoid us having to take such measures, please contact either T. Singleton or B. McKenzie before close of business on Tuesday afternoon. Yours sincerely, B. C. Rayne, Public Health Officer.' Ha ha ha . . . fuckin tubes!

John   Martin . . . you can prepare her for us. Chop her up Martin. I can cook. I can cook anything. We must eat her. For her goodness. We can have the thing inside if we eat her.

Martin   Aye, right! Get tae fuck you! D'ye hear him Tina, d'ye hear the cunt! You're fuckin tapped John. Dae it ma way and it's aboot profit. We can make dosh here. It's got tae profit. If ye want meat, I can get ye meat! The daft cunt's tapped!

Tina He's tapped, yeah. He wants to eat her, you only want to sell her to perverts who'll shag her. You're both fucking arseholes . . .

John No . . . we must consume her . . . to get the goodness . . . if we wait the goodness will be gone . . .

Tina Leave her! Leave her alone!

John She must be eaten . . . we must be one with her . . . we must be together . . . we need her goodness, our souls are dying . . .

Martin Naw! She's a resource John! She's mair use in the one piece! Have ye no been listening tae what I've been fuckin well telling ye aw these months! The market, ya daft cunt! The fuckin market.

Tina Leave her! You fucking sick, pathetic wankers! Leave her alone!

John Cook her . . . eat her . . .

Martin Sell her . . . fuck her . . .

Tina Leave her alone!

John Cook n eat . . . cook n eat . . .

Martin Sell n fuck . . . sell n fuck . . .

Tina Leave her alone . . . alone . . . alone . . .

These propositions are repeated as the cast pull apart then tentatively come together in a piece of physical theatre. **Tina**'*s voice becomes the stronger and more dominant as they share a shaky and fragile embrace.*

All Alone.

End

THE LEARNING CENTRE
HAMMERSMITH AND WEST
LONDON COLLEGE
GLIDDON ROAD
LONDON W14 9BL
0181 741 1688

IRVINE WELSH

Trainspotting

Read the No. 1 best-seller upon which the major film and long-running stage play were based.

'An unremitting powerhouse of a novel that marks the arrival of a major new talent. *Trainspotting* is a loosely knotted string of jagged, dislocated tales that lay bare the hearts of darkness of the junkies, wide-boys and psychos who ride the down escalator of opportunity in the nation's capital. Loud with laughter in the dark, this novel is the real McCoy. If you haven't heard of Irvine Welsh before . . . don't worry, you will.'

The Herald

'The voice of punk, grown up, grown wiser and grown eloquent'

Sunday Times

'A novel perpetually in a starburst of verbal energy – the stories we hear are retched from the gullet'

Scotland on Sunday

'*Trainspotting* marks the capital début of a capital writer. This marvellous novel might feel like a bad day in Bedlam, but boy is it exhilarating'

Jeff Torrington

'The best book ever written by man or woman . . . deserves to sell more copies than the Bible'

Rebel, Inc.

SHERMAN ALEXIE
Reservation Blues

Only Big Mom can help when you've made a deal with the Devil. Robert Johnson, legendary blues man, arrives at the Spokane Reservation looking for relief. Thomas Builds-the-Fire shows him the way and finds himself owner of the great man's guitar. So, with Victor Joseph, Junior Polatkin, and Chess and Checkers Warm Water, he hits the road, taking their four-and-a-half-chord rock and blues band to reservation bars, small town taverns and the urban landscapes of Seattle and Manhattan.

Reservation Blues is the mythic and musical tale of Coyote Springs, the best all-Indian, Catholic rock-and-roll band ever. With this powerful and poetic novel, Sherman Alexie is sure to further his reputation as 'one of the major lyric voices of our time' (*New York Times*).

'Hilarious but poignant, filled with enchantments but dead-on accurate with regard to modern Indian life, this *tour de force* will leave readers wondering if Alexie himself hasn't made a deal with the Gentleman in order to do everything so well'
Publisher's Weekly

'Blues as biting, sharp and timeless as any by Robert Johnson or Bessie Smith'
Kirkus

RUSSELL BANKS

Rule of the Bone

Rule of the Bone is an astonishing novel about a homeless youth living on the edge of society, a lost boy who maps the cruel world that surrounds him with mother-wit, humour and appalling honesty.

'*Rule of the Bone* is a magnificent book. I believed every word of it, forgot I was reading fiction. Russell Banks has created a story that is both shattering and reassuring, and a narrator, Bone, who will stay with me for the rest of my life'

Roddy Doyle

'Russell Banks presents without falsehood and with a tough affection the uncompromising moral voice of our time. In his work you find the craziness of false dreams, the political inequalities and, somehow, the sliver of redemption. I trust his portrait of America more than any other'

Michael Ondaatje

'If you've never read Russell Banks its time you acquired the habit'
Elmore Leonard

JAMES KELMAN

How late it was, how late

Winner of the 1994 Booker Prize

Sammy's had a bad week – most of it's just a blank space in his mind, and the bits that he can remember, he'd rather not. His wallet's gone, along with his new shoes; he's been arrested then beaten up by the police and thrown out on the street – and he's gone blind.

He remembers a row with his girlfriend, but she seems to have disappeared; and he might have been trying to fix a bit of business up with an old mate, but he's not too sure. Things aren't looking too good for Sammy, and his problems have hardly begun.

'Forging a wholly distinctive style from the bruised cadences of demotic Glaswegian, Kelman renders the hidden depths of ordinary lives in sardonic, abrasive prose which is more revealing of feelings than could ever be expected . . . as uplifting a novel as one could ever hope to read'

Sunday Telegraph

'*How late it was, how late* is gritty, realistic and bleak, but the overall tone is strangely positive. The fast pace of the narrative, Kelman's dry humour and . . . indomitable spirit combine to provide a liberating read'

Big Issue

'Beautiful, spirited thoughts hard up against the old brute truths . . . enormous artistic and social depth . . . James Kelman's best book yet'

Guardian

'A passionate, scintillating, brilliant song of a book'

Independent

EVELYN LAU

Fresh Girls

Evelyn Lau's bestselling autobiography, *Runaway of a Street Kid*, catapulted her from a life of teenage prostitution, phone sex and drug addition to award-winning fame. Now in her first work of fiction Lau moves deep into the world of women whose sexual experiences isolate them from the mainstream — women caught on the wrong side of Eros.

This is the world of fresh girls: Mary, a dominatrix who fantasises about her boyfriend while her clients beg at her feet; Jane, burnt out at twenty-four, who dreams of love and marriage but can't resist the feel of crisp fifty-dollar bills when she can get them; a young woman who goes to bed each night with the spikes of her metal bracelet cutting deep into her flesh. Turning tricks, donning leathers and wielding a whip become routine, while love and tenderness seem exotic to girls old before their time.

'*Fresh Girls* is told in cool, gleaming prose that echoes her hero Updike, although the subject matter could hardly be more different . . . short, sharp stories about the wilder shores of lust'
Tony Parsons, *Daily Telegraph*

'Each of Evelyn Lau's short stories . . . is shot through with pain — emotional physical and, in the case of all the sexual encounters that form the book's chill heart, both . . . These stories show love as a drug — and a deadly one at that'
Gill Morgan, *The Times*

ALINA REYES

The Butcher

A young girl goes to work in a butcher's shop during her college holiday. Every day the butcher whispers obscenities in her ear, describing their imagined love-making. And as the summer heat takes hold, so does her lust . . .

'Nothing short of staggering . . . an erotic *tour de force*; an exploration of raw sensuality – fleshy, beautiful and obscene. When you put it down, exhausted, you know you want to read it again'

Evening Standard

'This is not eroticism or soft-focus four-poster-bed sex. It is pornography, pure and simple. Utterly, absolutely, sexy . . . *The Butcher* has that crafted, stylised quality which compels the reader to linger and is another magnificent touch in the explosive build up of sexual tension. Its contents are guaranteed to disturb, unnerve and grip you; you will want to read it again and again'

Literary Review

'I never knew such going-on were even possible in a freezer . . . this is eroticism on a fantasy level which just about saves the book from obscenity. I think. But you have been warned'

Daily Express

'Alina Reyes' descriptions of an afternoon's love-making have an erotic force that leaves the Jilly Coopers and Jackie Collinses of this world cold . . . There are few more happily convincing arguments for sex as an aid to artistic creation than this succinct, evocative novel'

London Magazine

NTOZAKE SHANGE

Sassafrass, Cypress and Indigo

This is the story of three black girls and their mamma from
Charleston, South Carolina. Sassafrass, the eldest, is a poet and
weaver, living among Bohemians in Los Angeles and weaving a life
out of her work, her man, her memories and hopes. Cypress is a
dancer who leaves home to ease her inner turmoil. And Indigo, the
youngest, is still a child of Charleston who lives in poetry and has
the great gift of seeing the world's obvious magic – three girls who
must discover their dreams, desires and their rightful place within
black American culture.

'Shange's wit, lyricism and fierceness are marvellous'

New York Times

'Shange's voice is mesmerizing . . . Her characters are positive
forces, her novel full of universal truths'

Booklist

'Shange is a unique lyric singer . . . a mistress of colour, shape and
ringing, accurate imagery'

Washington Post

'A jubilant celebration of womanhood – as moving as the moon
. . . pure magic'

Kansas City Star

A Selected List of Fiction Available from Minerva

While every effort is made to keep prices low, it is sometimes necessary to increase prices at short notice. Mandarin Paperbacks reserves the right to show new retail prices on covers which may differ from those previously advertised in the text or elsewhere.

The prices shown below were correct at the time of going to press.

☐	7493 9513 3	**Reservation Blues**	Sherman Alexie	£6.99
☐	7493 9526 5	**Rule of the Bone**	Russell Banks	£5.99
☐	7493 9754 3	**Captain Corelli's Mandolin**	Louis de Bernières	£6.99
☐	7493 9947 3	**The Portable Virgin**	Anne Enright	£4.99
☐	7493 9883 3	**How late it was, how late**	James Kelman	£6.99
☐	7493 9620 2	**Fresh Girls**	Evelyn Lau	£4.99
☐	7493 9714 4	**The Lights Below**	Carl MacDougall	£5.99
☐	7493 9819 1	**Lemprière's Dictionary**	Lawrence Norfolk	£6.99
☐	7493 9875 2	**The Gifting Programme**	Sam North	£5.99
☐	7493 9984 8	**The Butcher**	Alina Reyes	£4.99
☐	7493 9035 2	**Sassafrass, Cypress and Indigo**	Ntozake Shange	£6.99
☐	7493 9606 7	**Trainspotting**	Irvine Welsh	£6.99

All these books are available at your bookshop or newsagent, or can be ordered direct from the address below. Just tick the titles you want and fill in the form below.

Cash Sales Department, PO Box 5, Rushden, Northants NN10 6YX.
Fax: 01933 414047 : Phone: 01933 414000.

Please send cheque, payable to 'Reed Book Services Ltd.', or postal order for purchase price quoted and allow the following for postage and packing:

£1.00 for the first book, 50p for the second; FREE POSTAGE AND PACKING FOR THREE BOOKS OR MORE PER ORDER.

NAME (Block letters)...

ADDRESS...

....

☐ I enclose my remittance for ....

☐ I wish to pay by Access/Visa Card Number ☐☐☐☐☐☐☐☐☐☐☐☐☐☐

Expiry Date ☐☐☐☐

Signature ....

Please quote our reference: MAND